OXFORD REVISION GU

CW00797209

GCSE

GEOGRAPHY
through diagrams

Garrett Nagle

Oxford University Press

Oxford University Press, Great Clarendon Street, Oxford OX2 6DP

Oxford New York
Athens Auckland Bangkok Bogota Bombay
Buenos Aires Calcutta Cape town Dar es Salaam Delhi
Florence Hong Kong Istanbul Karachi
Kuala Lumpur Madras Madrid Melbourne
Mexico City Nairobi Paris Singapore
Taipei Tokyo Toronto Warsaw

and associated companies in
Berlin Ibadan

Oxford is a trade mark of Oxford University Press

© **Garrett Nagle**

All rights reserved. This publication may not be reproduced,
stored or transmitted, in any forms or by any means, except in
accordance with the terms of licences issued by the Copyright
Licensing Agency, or except for fair dealing for the purposes
of research or private study, or criticism or review, as
permitted under the Copyright, Designs and Patents Act
1988. Enquiries concerning reproduction outside those terms
should be addressed to the Permissions Department, Oxford
University Press.

First published 1998

ISBN 0 19 913402 2 (Student's edition)
    0 19 913403 0 (Bookshop edition)

The publishers are grateful to Stanley Thornes (Publishers) Ltd for
permission to redraw and reproduce the diagrams at the bottom of
page 45 and on page 80. They come from *Skills and Techniques
in Geography* Nagle and Spencer, 1997.

Dedicated to Angela, Rosie, and Patrick

Typesetting, design and illustration by Hardlines, Charlbury, Oxford
Printed in Great Britain

CONTENTS

GCSE Geography syllabuses

MEG Geography Syllabus A (1586)

Content

Unit 1: People and the physical world
Plate tectonics
Rivers
Coasts

Unit 2: People and places to live
Population
Settlement

Unit 3: People and their needs
Quality of life
Economic activities
Energy

Unit 4: People and environment
Resource development and the local environment
The management of environments
The global environment

Scheme of Assessment

Foundation Tier

Paper 1	All units	2hr	45%
Paper 3	All units	$1\frac{1}{4}$ hr	30%
Coursework	–		25%

Higher Tier

Paper 2	All units	2hr	45%
Paper 4	All units	$1\frac{1}{4}$ hr	30%
Coursework	–		25%

MEG/WJEC Geography Syllabus B (Avery Hill) (1587)

Content/Options

Unit 1: Climate, the environment and people
Weather and climate
Natural environments

Unit 2: Water, landforms and people
The hydrosphere
Natural landforms
A study of a distinctive landform

Unit 3: People and place
Inequalities in urban areas
Improving the urban environment
Urban-rural interaction

Unit 4: People, work and development
Patterns of work and development
Work and development process

Scheme of Assessment

Foundation Tier

Paper 1	Three nominated units	$1\frac{3}{4}$ hr	45%
Paper 3	Problem solving - nominated unit*	$1\frac{1}{2}$ hr	30%
Coursework	–		25%

Higher Tier

Paper 2	Three nominated units	2hr	45%
Paper 4	Problem solving - nominated unit*	$1\frac{3}{4}$ hr	30%
Coursework	–		25%

*Each year units are nominated for each paper

MEG Geography Syllabus C (Bristol Project) (1588)

Content/Options

Theme 1: Physical systems and environments
a) Geomorphic processes and landforms
b) Atmospheric processes and climate
c) Physical environments and systems

Theme 2: Natural hazards and people
a) The nature and distribution of natural hazards
b) The processes responsible for natural hazards
c) The effects of natural hazards on people

Theme 3: Economic systems and development
a) Economic systems
b) Economic activity, growth and change
c) Internation disparities, trade and interdependence

Theme 4: Population and settlement
a) Population distribution, structure and change
b) The location and function of settlements
c) Land use within settlements
d) The growth and decline of settlements

Theme 5: People's use of the earth
a) The earth's resources
b) Exploitation and management of natural resources
c) Resolving issues

Scheme of Assessment

Foundation Tier

Paper 1	Places and themes	$2\frac{1}{4}$ hr	50%
Paper 3	Decision making exercise (module test)	$1\frac{1}{2}$ hr	25%
Coursework	–		25%

Higher Tier

Paper 2	Places and themes	$2\frac{1}{4}$ hr	50%
Paper 4	Decision making exercise (module test)	–	25%
Coursework	–		25%

NEAB Geography Syllabus A

Content/Options

Theme 1: The challenge of urban environments
Patterns and processes of urban growth
Patterns of land use
Dynamism in urban areas
The challenge of change in urban environments

Theme 2: Managing natural environments
Environmental systems
Managing the living world

Theme 3: The impact of economic change
What is economic change?
changes in the location of economic activity
Economic growth and decline

Scheme of Assessment

Paper 1 (Foundation and Higher)	1hr	25%
Paper 2 (Foundation and Higher)	2hr	50%
Coursework	–	25%

NEAB Geography Syllabus B

Content/Options

The United Kingdom
Urban growth and change
The farm as a system
Electricity generation
Water resources
Factors affecting the location of manufacturing industry
Tourism
Ports
Road transport

The European Union
Farming in Southern Italy
The Ruhr Conurbation and its changing industrial development
Tourism in Mediterranean Spain
The Rhine Waterway
The growth of Rotterdam/Europort

The wider world
Amazonia
Ganges Delta (India and Bangladesh)
Japan

Scheme of Assessment

Paper 1 (Foundation and Higher)	$1\frac{1}{2}$ hr	35%
Paper 2 (Foundation and Higher)	2hr	40%
Coursework	–	25%

NEAB Geography Syllabus C

Content/Options

Key Area A: Natural hazards
Unstable plate margins
Storms
River floods

Key Area B: Fragile environments
Disappearing tropical rain forests
Soil damage
Threatened natural landscapes in the UK

Key Area C: Population issues
Famine and starvation
Ageing populations
International migration

Key Area D: Urban issues
Pressures at the rural-urban fringe
Inner cities
Urban transport

Key Area E: Resource issues
Water supply
Resource depletion
Power generation in the UK

Key Area F: Development issues
Unequal development
Swing to services
A new agricultural revolution

Scheme of Assessment

Foundation Tier

Paper 1 (Foundation) Issues evaluation exercise	$1\frac{1}{2}$ hr	25%
Paper 2 (Foundation)	$1\frac{1}{2}$ hr	50%
Coursework	–	25%

Higher Tier

Paper 1 (Higher) Issues evaluation exercise	$1\frac{1}{2}$ hr	25%
Paper 2 (Higher)	$1\frac{3}{4}$ hr	50%
Coursework	–	25%

SEG Geography Syllabus A (2000)

Content/Options
'Physical' topics
THREE from:
1. Tectonic activity
2. Rocks and landscapes
3. Ice
4. Rivers
5. Coasts
6. Weather and climate
7. Ecosystems

'Human' topics
ONE from:
1. Population
2. Settlement

ONE from:
3. Agriculture
4. Industry

ONE from:
5. Managing resources and tourism
6. Development and interdependence

Scheme of Assessment

Written Component One	$1\frac{3}{4}$ hr	40%
Written Component Two	$1\frac{1}{2}$ hr	35%
Coursework	–	25%

SEG Geography Syllabus B (2050)

Content/Options
Topic A: People and urban change
Population distribution
Towns and cities
Migration and urban growth

Topic B: Leisure, recreation and tourism
Tourism and the economy
The provision of leisure activities
The management of recreation and tourism environments

Topic C: The physical environment
Atmospheric processes and climate
Tectonic activity
Water

Topic D: Economic development
Levels of development
Changing levels of economic activity
Economic and environmental pressures

Scheme of Assessment

Written Component One	$1\frac{1}{2}$ hr	25%
Written Component Two	2hr	50%
Coursework	–	25%

London Geography Syllabus A (1310)

Content/Options
Theme A: People and places
A1 - Population
A2 - Settlement

Theme B: People and work
B3 - Agriculture
B4 - Industry

Theme C: Landscapes - challenge and management
C5 - Coastal landscapes
C6 - Valley landscapes

Theme D: Environmental systems
ONE from:
D7 - Water, weather and climate
D8 - Soils, vegetation and ecosystems

Scheme of Assessment
Foundation Tier

Paper 1	1hr	25%
Paper 2	2hr	50%
Coursework	–	25%

Higher Tier

Paper 3	1hr	25%
Paper 4	2hr	50%
Coursework	–	25%

London Geography Syllabus B (1311)

Content/Options
Theme 1: Issues in natural environments
1.1 - The drainage basin
1.2 - Coastal management
1.3 - Environmental hazards

Theme 2: Issues in rural environments
2.1 - Primary activities and the rural environment
2.2 - Recreation and the rural environment
2.3 - Rural-urban links

Theme 3: Issues in economic development

Theme 4: Issues in urban environments
4.1 - The internal structure of urban areas
4.2 - Journeys within and between urban areas
4.3 - Changes in urban population

Scheme of Assessment
Foundation Tier

Paper 1		2hr	50%
Paper 2	Decision-making exercise	$1\frac{1}{4}$ hr	25%
Coursework		–	25%

Higher Tier

Paper 3		2hr	50%
Paper 4	Decision-making exercise	$1\frac{1}{4}$ hr	25%
Coursework		–	25%

WJEC Geography Syllabus A

Content/Options
Unit 1: The fragile world - physical systems and environmental issues
1A - Ice, rivers and the sea create distinctive landscapes
1B - There are distinctive patterns of weather and climate
1C - The physical environment may affect or, in turn, be affected by human activities. Both sets of effects have to be managed.
1D - Exploitation of a fragile environment may have far reaching consequences

Unit 2: The interdependent world - socio-economic activities, global inequalities and places
2A - Different areas have different economic activities which, over time, change in character and location with social consequences
2B - Economic and social change influence urban development
2C - There is increasing global interdependence through trade
2D - Global inequalities exist in the balance between population and resources

Scheme of Assessment

Paper 1	Unit 1	$1\frac{3}{4}$ hr	40%
Paper 2	Unit 2	$1\frac{3}{4}$ hr	40%
Coursework		–	20%

GCSE (Short Course) Geography Syllabuses

MEG (Short Course) Geography (3580)

Content/Options
Section 1: Physical
Unit 1   Hydrological themes
Unit 2   Environmental themes

Section 2: Human
Unit 3   Economic themes Populations
Unit 4   Urban themes

Scheme of Assessment
Foundation Tier

Paper 1	All units	2hr	75%
Coursework		–	25%

Higher Tier

Paper 2	All units	2hr	75%
Coursework		–	25%

NEAB (Short Course) Geography Syllabus A

Content/Options
Theme 1: Living in cities
Dynamism in urban areas
The challenge of change in urban environments

Theme 2: Living in the natural world
Environmental systems
Managing the living world

Theme 3: Living with economic change
Economic growth and decline

Scheme of Assessment

Written Paper (Foundation and Higher)	1hr 25m	75%
Coursework	–	25%

SEG (Short Course) Geography (1420)

Content/Options
Section A - Environmental Issues
Section B - 'Physical' topics
ONE from:
Ice
Rivers
Coasts

Section C: 'Human' topics
ONE from:
Settlement
Agriculture
Development and interdependence

Scheme of Assessment

Written Component	$1\frac{1}{2}$ hr	75%
Coursework	–	25%

Revision tips

1. First of all you must know what the exam consists of. If you have not already got past papers, you can order some from the Exam Boards. For this you need to know your Exam Board and the Syllabus number. It is very useful to have a selection of past papers, and if you write to the Board at the address given below, ask for the most recent papers. Also ask if there have been any changes to the Syllabus, for example the new 1998 examinations, and ask for a copy of the specimen paper.

2. Study the past papers and familiarise yourself with the layout of the paper.

3. Revise in short manageable chunks; do not attempt to do all of the subject in one go, but take each topic in turn.

4. When you revise, use whichever method or methods you feel most happy with. These could include:
   - Highlighter pens
   - Lists and rhymes
   - Note cards
   - Mnemonics (the first letter of words, e.g. CASH standing for corrosion, abrasion, solution and hydraulic impact, ie. the types of erosion in a river or at the coast)

5. Have regular breaks; it is difficult to concentrate for more than forty minutes at a time. Have a fifteen minute break first of all. After the next forty minutes take a longer break. Then after the next forty minutes take a shorter break and so on.

6. Test yourself. This could be writing answers to past questions, drawing sketch maps, learning facts and figures, identifying symbols on an ordnance survey map etc. Ask a teacher, parent or friend to assess you. If you ask a friend, then two of you are revising and helping each other's work. This is very often the best method.

7. Reward yourself with a treat.

8. Do not work too late, get plenty of sleep, and try to stay fresh.

9. Work to a revision timetable - it is best if you have a timetable plotted and keep to it. This needs to take into account when your exams are in all other subjects.

Addresses of the Exam Boards

SOUTHERN EXAMINING GROUP
Stag Hill House
Guildford
Surrey   GU2 5XJ

LONDON EXAMINATIONS (Edexcel)
Stewart House
32 Russell Square
London   WC1B 5DN

MIDLAND EXAMINING GROUP
Syndicate Buildings
1 Hills Road
Cambridge   CB1 2EU

NORTHERN EXAMINATIONS & ASSESSMENT BOARD
Devas Street
Manchester   M15 6EX

Plate tectonics

Plate tectonics is a set of theories which describes and explains the distribution of earthquakes, volcanoes, fold mountains, and continental drift. It states that the earth's core consists of semi-molten magma (superheated semi-liquid rock), and that the earth's surface or crust moves around on the magma. The cause of the movement is radioactive decay in the core. This creates huge **convection currents** in the magma, which rise towards the earth's surface, drag continents apart, and cause them to collide.

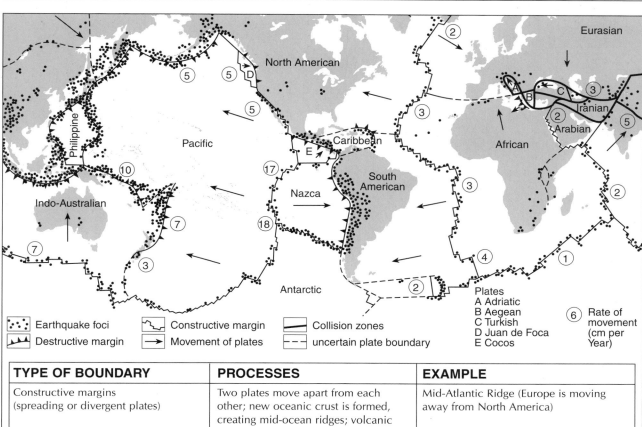

Earthquake foci · Constructive margin | Collision zones
Destructive margin | Movement of plates | uncertain plate boundary

Plates
A Adriatic
B Aegean
C Turkish
D Juan de Foca
E Cocos

⑥ Rate of movement (cm per Year)

TYPE OF BOUNDARY	PROCESSES	EXAMPLE
Constructive margins (spreading or divergent plates)	Two plates move apart from each other; new oceanic crust is formed, creating mid-ocean ridges; volcanic activity is common	Mid-Atlantic Ridge (Europe is moving away from North America)
Destructive margins (subduction zone)	The oceanic crust moves towards the the continental crust and sinks beneath it due to its greater density; deep sea trenches and island arcs are formed; volcanic activity is common	Nazca sinks under the South American plate.
Collision zones	Two continental crusts collide: as neither can sink they are folded up into fold mountains	The Indian plate collided with the Eurasian plate to form the Himalayas
Conservative margins (passive margins or transform plates)	Two plates move sideways past each other but land is neither destroyed nor created	San Andreas fault in California

THE EVIDENCE FOR PLATE TECTONICS
The evidence to support the theories of plate tectonics includes
- the 'fit' of the continents (North America, South America and Africa as shown in the diagram)
- glacial deposits in Brazil match those in West Africa
- the geological sequence in India matches that of Antarctica
- fossil remains of an early reptile, mesosaurus, are found only in Brazil and the south west of Africa
- the reversal of magnetic particles is similar in rocks either side of the mid ocean ridges.

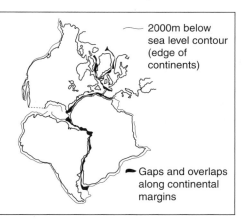

— 2000m below sea level contour (edge of continents)

— Gaps and overlaps along continental margins

Volcanoes

A volcano is an opening through the earth's crust through which magma, molten rock, and ash are erupted onto the land.

Volcanoes tend to be conical in shape, although there are a variety of forms depending upon

- the nature of the material erupted
- the type of eruption
- the amount of change since the eruption.

Most volcanoes are located at the edges of plate boundaries, although some are found in the interior of plates.

PREDICTING VOLCANOES

Scientists are increasingly successful in predicting volcanoes. Since 1980 they have correctly predicted 19 of Mt. St. Helens' 22 eruptions and Alaska's Redoubt volcano in 1989. However, there have been false alarms: in 1976 72,000 residents of Guadaloupe were forced to leave their homes, and, in 1980, Mammoth Lake in California suffered from a reduction in tourist numbers owing to mounting concern regarding volcanic activity.

The main ways of prediction include

- seismometers to record swarms of tiny earthquakes that occur as the magma rises
- chemical sensors to measure increased sulphur levels
- lasers to detect the physical swelling of the volcano, and
- ultra sound to monitor low frequency waves in the magma, resulting from the surge of gas and molten rock, as happened at Pinatubo, El Chichon and Mt. St. Helens.

CASE STUDY: MOUNT PINATUBO

Details: 9th June 1991; eruption after 600 years; between 12th and 15th June ash and rock was scattered over a radius of 100 km; killed 350 people and made 200,000 people homeless, largely due to mudslides.

Effects: Mudslides covered 50,000 ha of cropland and destroyed 200,000 homes; 600,000 people lost their jobs.

Causes:

a   Earthquake 16th July 1990 (7.7 on Richter Scale; 1600 dead)

b   Basalt from the upper mantle squeezed into the magma chamber of the dormant volcano

c   Basalt reactivated viscous lava and created gas-charged magma (andesite)

d   This rose towards the surface causing volcano to bulge

e   Pressure blasted away the dome spewing 20 million tonnes of material into the atmosphere

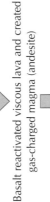

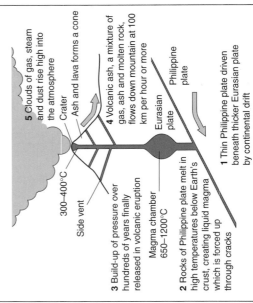

5 Clouds of gas, steam and dust rise high into the atmosphere

Crater

Ash and lava forms a cone

300–400°C

Side vent

4 Volcanic ash, a mixture of gas, ash and molten rock, flows down mountain at 100 km per hour or more

3 Build-up of pressure over hundreds of years finally released in volcanic eruption

Magma chamber 650–1200°C

2 Rocks of Philippine plate melt in high temperatures below Earth's crust, creating liquid magma which is forced up through cracks

Eurasian plate

Philippine plate

1 Thin Philippine plate driven beneath thicker Eurasian plate by continental drift

---

United States
Mt Baker (1870)
Mt St Helens (1980)
Lassen Park (1917)

Mexico
Mt Paricutin (1943)
Mt Chichon (1982)

Japan
Mt Unzen (1991)

Philippines
Mt Pinatubo (1991)

North American Plate

Martinique
Mt Pelée (1902)

Colombia
Nevado de Ruiz (1985)

Antarctic Plate

Ring of fire

Pacific Plate pushing under Philippine Plate

Pacific Plate

Molten magma bubbling up from interior of planet causing Pacific Plate to expand

Eurasian Plate

Philippine Plate

Indo-Australian Plate

Bali
Mt Agung (1963)

Java
Krakatoa (1883)

THE PACIFIC RING OF FIRE

Three-quarters of the earth's 550 historically active volcanoes lie along the Pacific Ring of Fire. This includes most of the world's recent eruptions, including Mount Pinatubo in the Philippines, which erupted in 1991. Without volcanic activity the Philippines would not exist: they comprise the remains of previous eruptions.

2 Geology and rocks

Earthquakes

An earthquake is a sudden, violent movement of the earth. They occur after a build up of pressure causes rocks to give way. Most earthquakes are found at plate boundaries but others are caused by

- nuclear testing
- drilling for oil
- the weight of large dams
- coal mining.

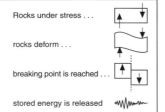

Rocks under stress . . .

rocks deform . . .

breaking point is reached . . .

stored energy is released

EARTHQUAKE PREDICTION

There are a number of ways of predicting and monitoring earthquakes. These include

- crustal movement
- changes in electrical conductivity
- historic evidence
- strange and unusual animal behaviour.

WORLD DISTRIBUTION OF EARTHQUAKES

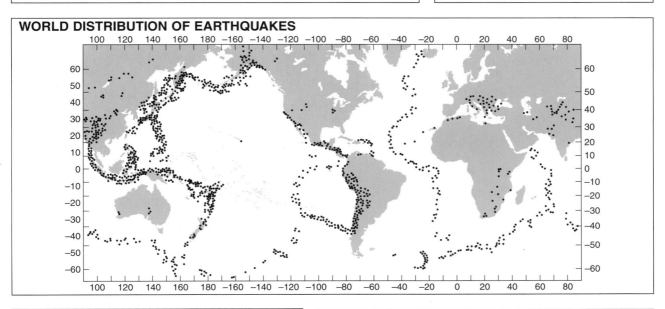

CASE STUDY: THE KOBE EARTHQUAKE

The Kobe earthquake on the 17th January 1995 killed over 5,000 people, injured over 30, 000, and made almost 750, 000 homeless. It was caused by the subduction (undercutting) of the Philippine Plate underneath the Eurasian Plate. Kobe is situated near the northern end of the Philippine Plate.

Conditions were made worse by rain and strong winds. These increased the risk of landslides. Damp, unhygienic conditions encouraged disease. Fires, broken glass, broken water pipes, and a lack of insurance meant that many people lost their livelihoods.

EARTHQUAKE DAMAGE

The factors affecting earthquake damage include

- population density
- the nature and type of buildings
- the time of day
- the distance from the centre (epicentre) of the earthquake
- the type of rocks and sediments
- the strength of the earthquake
- secondary hazards (those that happen after, but because of, the main hazard) such as mudslides and tsunami (tidal waves).

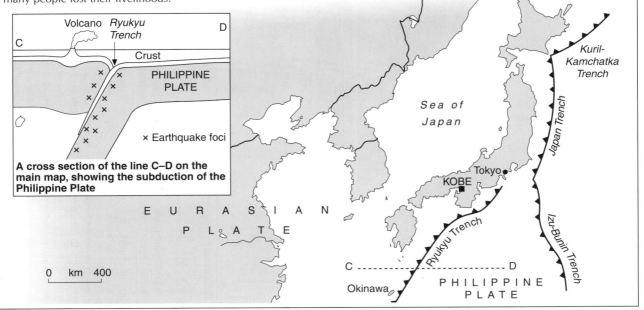

A cross section of the line C–D on the main map, showing the subduction of the Philippine Plate

Rocks and relief

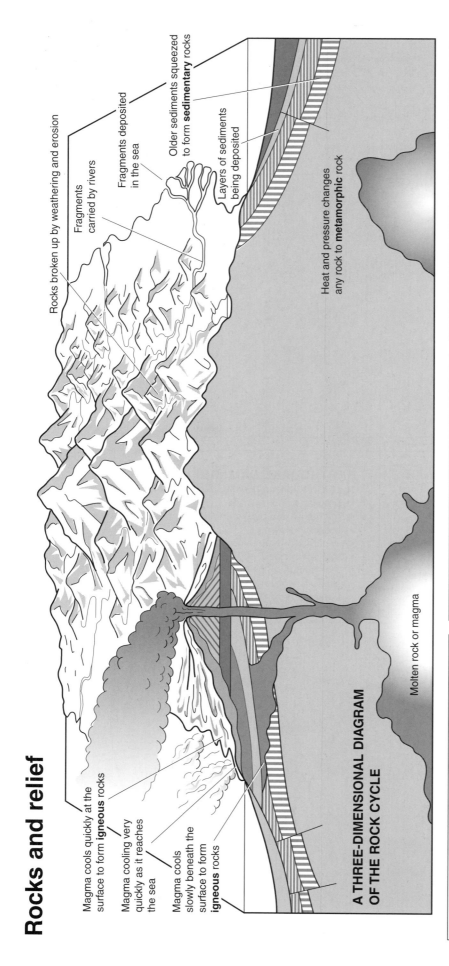

Rocks broken up by weathering and erosion

Fragments carried by rivers

Fragments deposited in the sea

Older sediments squeezed to form **sedimentary** rocks

Layers of sediments being deposited

Heat and pressure changes any rock to **metamorphic** rock

Magma cools quickly at the surface to form **igneous** rocks

Magma cooling very quickly as it reaches the sea

Magma cools slowly beneath the surface to form **igneous** rocks

Molten rock or magma

A THREE-DIMENSIONAL DIAGRAM OF THE ROCK CYCLE

Sedimentary rocks are formed from fragments of older rocks and organic material. They are squeezed together to form solid rock, such as sandstone and limestone.

Metamorphic rocks are formed by intense heat and pressure. This changes existing rocks. Marble is a good example.

Igneous rocks are formed by the cooling of molten magma. Granite and basalt are good examples.

Rocks vary in terms of their strength and their permeability (the ability to transmit water). The **strength** determines whether they produce highlands or lowlands, whereas the **permeability** determines to what extent the landscape is wet at the surface or dry. Carboniferous limestone gives dry upland areas, whereas clay produces wet lowland areas.

ROCK PERMEABILITY AND HARDNESS

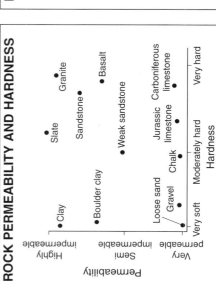

Permeability

Highly impermeable
Semi impermeable
Very permeable

Clay
Boulder clay
Loose sand
Gravel
Chalk
Slate
Sandstone
Weak sandstone
Granite
Basalt
Jurassic limestone
Carboniferous limestone

Very soft
Moderately hard
Very hard

Hardness

ROCK FEATURES – HARDNESS AND PERMEABILITY

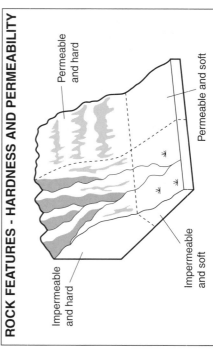

Permeable and hard

Permeable and soft

Impermeable and soft

Impermeable and hard

Weathering

Weathering is the **decomposition** and **disintegration** of rocks **in situ**, that is without any movement involved. Decomposition refers to chemical weathering and creates altered rock substances. By contrast, disintegration, or mechanical weathering, produces smaller, angular fragments of the same rock. Weathering is important for landscape evolution as it breaks down rock and facilitates erosion and transport.

Mechanical (physical) weathering

There are four main types of mechanical weathering: freeze-thaw (ice crystal growth), salt crystal growth, disintegration, and pressure release.

Freeze-thaw occurs when water in joints and cracks freezes at 0°C and expands by 10%. This is enough to crack and split most rocks. It is most effective in environments where there is lots of moisture and there are frequent fluctuations above and below freezing point. Hence it is very common in arctic and mountainous regions.

Temperature above freezing

Temperature below freezing

Rainwater trickles into joints   Ice expands forcing joints to widen

Disintegration is found in hot desert areas where there is a large diurnal (day and night) temperature range. Rocks heat up by day and contract by night. As rock is a poor conductor of heat, stresses occur only in the outer layers and cause peeling or exfoliation to occur. A little moisture is essential for this to happen.

Chemical weathering

There are four main types of chemical weathering: carbonation-solution, hydrolysis, hydration, and oxidation.

Hydrolysis occurs on rocks with feldspar such as granite. Feldspar reacts with acid water and forms kaolin (or china clay). Other minerals in the granite, such as quartz and mica, remain with the kaolin.

Oxidation occurs when iron compounds react with oxygen to produce a reddish brown coating.

Hydration is the process whereby certain minerals absorb water, expand and change.

Carbonation-solution occurs on rocks with calcium carbonate, e.g. chalk and limestone. Rain-fall and dissolved carbon dioxide form a weak carbonic acid. (Organic acids acidify water too.) Calcium carbonate reacts with acid water and forms calcium bicarbonate, which is soluble and is removed by percolating water.

Bedding planes are horizontal layers of sedimentary rock

Joints are vertical cracks in sedimentary rocks

Pressure release is the process whereby overlying rocks are removed by erosion thereby causing underlying ones to expand and fracture. The removal of a great weight, such as a glacier, has the same effect.

Salt crystal growth occurs in areas where temperatures fluctuate around 26-28°C, causing salts to expand by 300%. When water evaporates, salt crystals may be left behind to attack rocks. Salt crystal growth is common in hot desert regions.

Limestone landscapes

LIMESTONE AREAS IN THE BRITISH ISLES

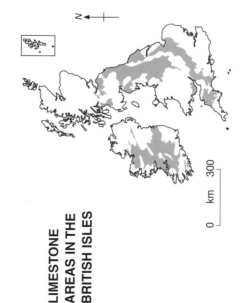

0 km 300

N

LIMESTONE SCENERY

Limestone scenery is unique, because of its

- permeability and
- solubility in rain and ground-water.

Variations exist between the different types of limestone because of their hardness, chemical composition, jointing, and bedding planes.

There are three main types of contrasting limestone scenery in the UK

1. Carboniferous limestone (220-280 million years old), such as the Mendips and the Pennines
2. Jurassic limestone (120-150 million years old), such as the Cotswolds
3. Cretaceous limestone or chalk (70-100 million years old), such as the North and South Downs.

Limestone consists of mainly $CaCO_3$ (Calcium Carbonate). It is formed from the remains of organic matter, notably plants and shells. Owing to its permeability, limestone areas are often dry on the surface and are known as Karst areas (from the Yugoslav krs meaning dry). Karst features are best developed on carboniferous limestone because of its greater strength, and its lower porosity and permeability compared with other limestones.

Carboniferous limestone has a distinctive bedding plane and joint pattern, known as **massively jointed**. These act as weaknesses allowing water to percolate into the rock and dissolve it. One of the main processes to affect limestone is carbonation-solution.

SURFACE FEATURES

Large areas of bare exposed limestone are known as **limestone pavements**. Good examples include the Burren, County Clare, and at Malham, Yorkshire. As the joints and cracks are attacked and enlarged over thousands of years, the permeability increases. **Clints** (clumps of rock) and **grikes** (gaps between the rocks) develop on the surface of the exposed limestone. **Karren** or **lapies** are small scale solution grooves, only a few centimetres deep, caused by runoff and solution on limestone.

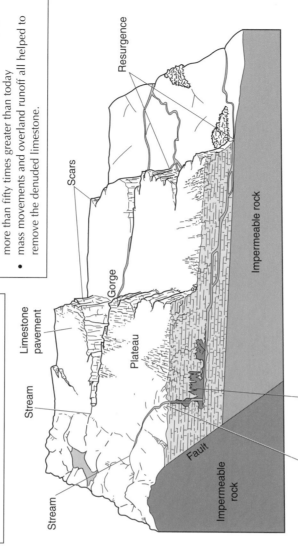

Stream

Limestone pavement

Scars

Plateau

Gorge

Resurgence

Impermeable rock

Fault

Impermeable rock

Cavern with stalactites and stalagmites

Swallow hole

Stream

Other important surface features include dry valleys such as Cheddar Gorge. A dry valley is a river valley without a river and is a common feature on chalk and limestone. It is likely that the Gorge was formed by surface streams during cold periglacial phases. Intense weathering, erosion and mass movements took place during this period

- freeze thaw was rapid, helped by the numerous exposed joints and bedding planes
- carbonation was increased owing to the increased solubility of CO_2 with low temperatures
- snowmelt caused river discharges to rise to a level more than fifty times greater than today
- mass movements and overland runoff all helped to remove the denuded limestone.

Swallow holes

Swallow holes (or **sinks**) are smaller depressions in the landscape, also caused by the solution of limestone. In addition, they can be formed by the enlargement of a grike system, by carbonation or river activity, or by the collapse of a cavern such as Gaping Ghyll near Malham. Often a river disappears down the hole, hence the term 'sink'.

Resurgent streams

Resurgent streams arise when the limestone lies on top of an impermeable rock, such as clay. A good example is the River Axe at Wookey Hole.

Underground features include caves and tunnels formed by carbonation-solution and erosion by rivers. **Stalactites** develop from the top of the cave, whereas **stalagmites** are formed on the base of the cave. Rates of deposition are slow, about 1 mm every 100 yrs (the thickness of a coat of paint). The speed at which water drips from the cave ceiling appears to have some influence on whether stalactites (slow drip) or stalagmites (fast drip) are formed.

Chalk and clay landscapes

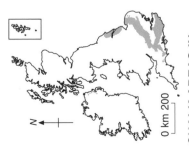

CHALK AREAS IN THE BRITISH ISLES

0 km 200

N

CHALK

Unlike carboniferous limestone, which is hard, grey, angular and jointed, chalk is soft, white, rounded and porous. Chalk in southern England is best illustrated by the escarpments of the North and South Downs. Other main types of chalk slopes are the Hogsback of Dorset and Guildford, and the flat Salisbury Plain. However, there are other famous chalk landforms such as the Folkestone Warren, the Seven Sisters, and the Needles.

Escarpments are not unique to chalk, but they are generally most easily identified on chalk. They have a steep **scarp** slope and a gentle **dip** slope. The steepness of the scarp slope depends upon weathering, erosion and mass movement on the slope and removal by a river at the base. Sometimes escarpments are called **cuestas**.

Dry valleys, such as Scratchy Bottom near Lulworth Cove and the Devil's Dyke near Brighton, are common, especially on dip slopes. In some cases, such as in the Vale of the White Horse, Uffington, periglacial avalanches have been suggested as a mechanism for their formation.

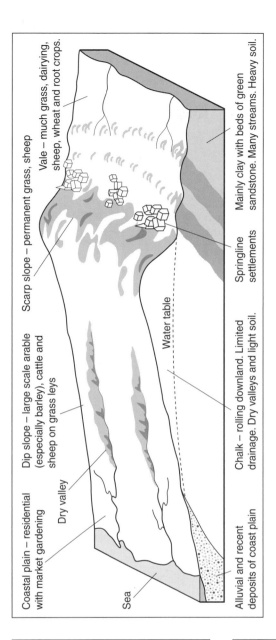

Coastal plain – residential with market gardening

Dip slope – large scale arable (especially barley), cattle and sheep on grass leys

Scarp slope – permanent grass, sheep

Vale – much grass, dairying, sheep, wheat and root crops.

Dry valley

Water table

Sea

Alluvial and recent deposits of coast plain

Chalk – rolling downland. Limited drainage. Dry valleys and light soil.

Springline settlements

Mainly clay with beds of green sandstone. Many streams. Heavy soil.

SLOPES

Steeply dipping, e.g. Hogsback near Guildford

Clay

Chalk
Hogsback

Clay

Gently dipping, e.g. North Downs

Dip slope

Scarp

Escarpment

Horizontal strata, e.g. Salisbury Plain

Plain or Plateau

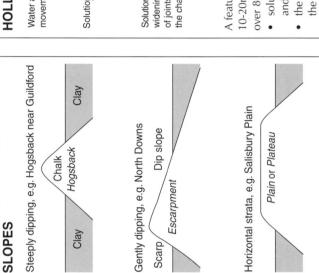

HOLLOWS IN CHALK

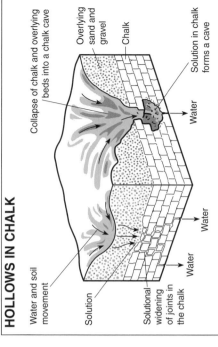

Collapse of chalk and overlying beds into a chalk cave

Overlying sand and gravel

Chalk

Water and soil movement

Solution

Solutional widening of joints in the chalk

Solution in chalk forms a cave

Water

Water

Water

A feature very common in Dorset's heathlands are hollows, generally 10-20m wide and 3-4m deep. However one, Culpepper's Dish, is over 80m wide and 20m deep. Two explanations are
- solution at the boundary of the chalk and the overlaying material and
- the collapse of a small cave system in the chalk and the sinking of the overlaying beds.

CLAY

Clay is a fine grained, soft rock that is easily eroded. It is the end result of chemical weathering and river erosion. Clay is very porous but it is impermeable. It is impermeable because when it is wet the individual particles expand (hydrate) and pack very tightly. This seals off the surface and makes it impermeable. Because of its softness, clay forms undulating lowlands with lots of surface drainage, such as rivers, marshes and moors. When drained, clay provides fertile soils, such as those in East Anglia. Settlements are usually found on the higher ground to avoid the risk of flooding. The villages on the edge of Otmoor near Oxford are a good example.

Granite landscapes

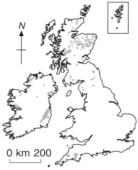

0 km 200

GRANITE

Granite is an igneous, crystalline rock. It has great physical strength and is very resistant to erosion. There are many types of granite but all share certain characteristics. They contain quartz, mica and felspar. These are resistant minerals. The main processes of weathering that occur on granite are freeze-thaw and hydrolysis.

Characteristic granite landscapes include exposed large-scale **batholiths**, which form mountains. Good examples include the Wicklow Mountains and the Mountains of Mourne. **Tors** are isolated masses of bare rock. They can be up to 20m high, such as Hay Tor and Yes Tor. Some of the boulders of the mass are attached to part of the bedrock. Others merely rest on the top.

Bodmin Moor is one exposure of a **granitic dome** in the South West peninsula. Denudation (any wearing away of the earth's surface) has slowly removed rocks to expose the

granite masses. Due to their greater resistance, the granite has remained on upland areas.

Due to granite's resistance, weathering results in a thin, gritty soil cover. Such soils are generally infertile, so rough grazing is the dominant land use. Granite is an impermeable rock and many marshy hollows at the heads of the valleys indicate the limited downward movement of water.

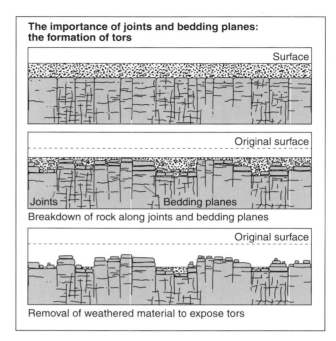

The importance of joints and bedding planes: the formation of tors

Surface

Original surface

Joints — Bedding planes

Breakdown of rock along joints and bedding planes

Original surface

Removal of weathered material to expose tors

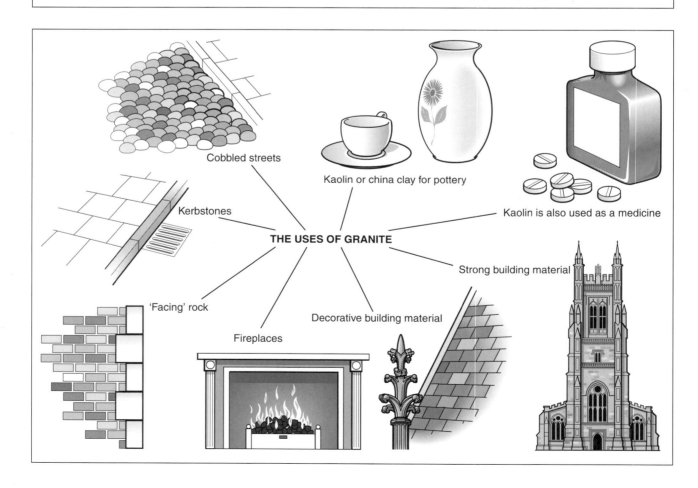

Cobbled streets

Kerbstones

'Facing' rock

Fireplaces

Kaolin or china clay for pottery

Kaolin is also used as a medicine

THE USES OF GRANITE

Strong building material

Decorative building material

The uses of rocks

Rocks are used for many things. For example in a house there are many different types of rocks that are used. In old houses stone was used for the walls and slate was used for the roof. New houses are mostly built of bricks (from clay) and concrete. Clay can be moulded into different shapes when it is heated and is, therefore, a useful material for building. The foundations of a house are made of concrete. This is a mixture of crushed rock (called aggregate), cement, sand and gravel.

The walls of a house are covered by plaster. This is made from the mineral gypsum. Cement or mortar is a mixture of powdered limestone, clay, and sand.

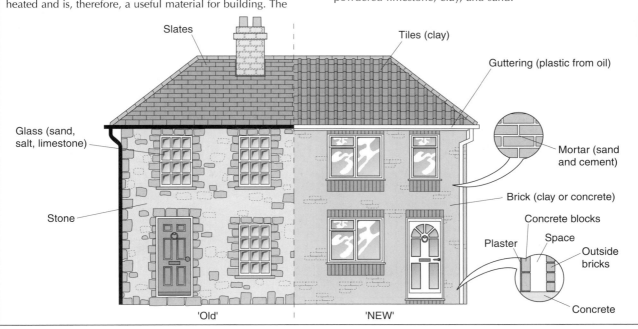

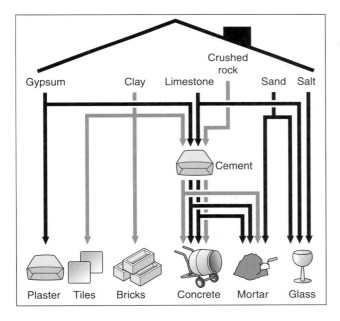

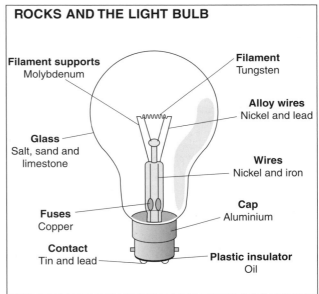

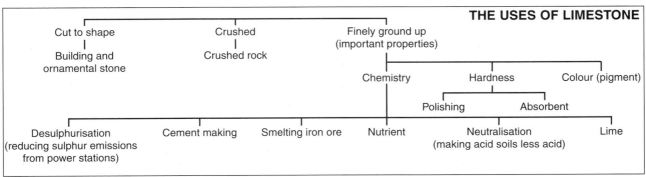

The hydrological cycle and river regimes

Hydrology is the study of water.
Precipitation includes all forms of rainfall, snow, frost, hail, and dew. It is the conversion and transfer of moisture in the atmosphere to the land.
Interception is the precipitation that is collected and stored by vegetation.
Overland runoff is water that flows over the land's surface.
Infiltration is water that seeps into the ground.
Evaporation refers to water from the ground or a lake that changes into a gas.
Transpiration is water loss from vegetation to the atmosphere.
Evapotranspiration (EVT) is the combined losses of transpiration and evaporation.

The **hydrological cycle** is the movement of water between air, land, and sea. It varies from place to place and over time. The hydrological cycle in the Arctic is very different from that in the Mediterranean. The hydrological cycle in winter in Britain is very different from the summer.

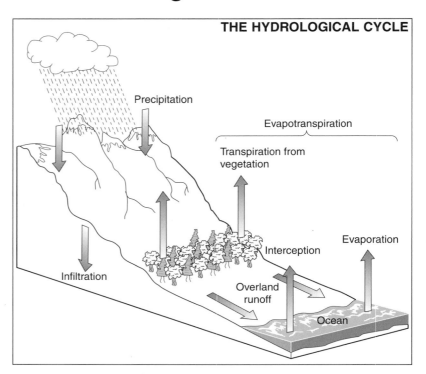

THE HYDROLOGICAL CYCLE

RIVER REGIMES

A **river regime** is the annual variation in the flow of a river. In Britain river flows are higher in winter for a number of reasons
- higher rainfall
- lower temperatures and hence lower EVT
- less interception by deciduous vegetation.

By contrast, in summer there is
- less rainfall
- higher temperatures and more EVT
- greater interception by deciduous vegetation.

In general, river regimes reflect climate. It is possible to have complex regimes. For example, some rivers flow through a variety of climate types, and others have tributaries from different climates.

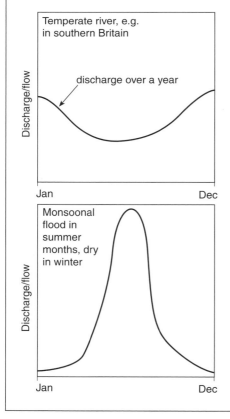

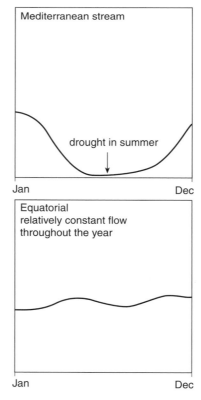

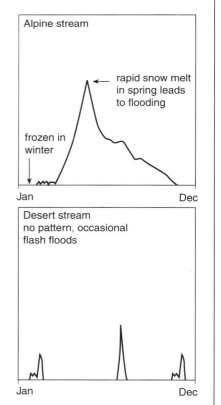

Storm hydrographs

A **storm hydrograph** shows us how a river changes over a short period, such as a day or a couple of days. Usually it is drawn to show how a river reacts to an individual storm. Each storm hydrograph has a series of parts.

The **rising limb** shows us how quickly the flood waters begin to rise.

The **peak flow** is the maximum discharge of the river as a result of the storm.

The **time lag** is the time between the height of the storm (not the start or the end) and the maximum flow in the river.

The **recessional limb** is the speed at which the water level in the river declines after the peak.

Baseflow is the normal level of the river, which is fed by groundwater.

Quickflow or **stormflow** is the water which gets into the river as a result of overland runoff.

Flood hydrographs are affected by a number of factors
- climate (rainfall total, intensity, and seasonality increase flooding)
- soils (impermeable clay soils create more flooding)
- vegetation (vegetation intercepts rainfall and so flooding is less likely)
- infiltration capacity (soils with a low infiltration capacity cause much overland runoff)
- rock type (permeable rocks will allow water to infiltrate, thereby reducing the flood peak)
- slope angle (on steeper slopes there is greater runoff)
- drainage density (the more stream channels that there are, the more water gets into rivers)
- human impact (creating impermeable surfaces and additional drainage channels increases the risk of flooding).

Urban hydrographs are different to rural ones. They have
- a shorter time lag
- a steeper rising limb
- a higher peak flow
- a steeper recessional limb.

This is because there are more impermeable surfaces in urban areas (roofs, pavements, roads, buildings) as well as more drainage channels (gutters, drains, sewers).

READING A STORM HYDROGRAPH

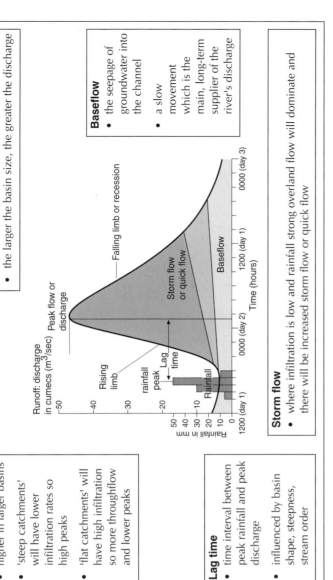

Discharge peak
- higher in larger basins
- 'steep catchments' will have lower infiltration rates so high peaks
- 'flat catchments' will have high infiltration so more throughflow and lower peaks

Lag time
- time interval between peak rainfall and peak discharge
- influenced by basin shape, steepness, stream order

Hydrograph size (area under the graph)
- the higher the rainfall, the greater the discharge
- the larger the basin size, the greater the discharge

Baseflow
- the seepage of groundwater into the channel
- a slow movement which is the main, long-term supplier of the river's discharge

Storm flow
- where infiltration is low and rainfall strong overland flow will dominate and there will be increased storm flow or quick flow

URBAN HYDROLOGY AND THE STORM HYDROGRAPH

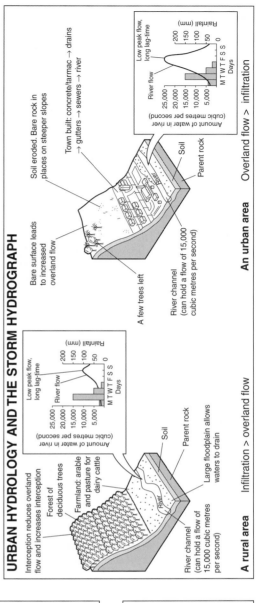

A rural area — Infiltration > overland flow

An urban area — Overland flow > infiltration

River erosion and transport

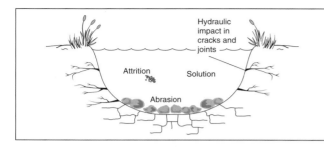

RIVER EROSION

Abrasion is the wearing away of the river bed and bank by the load carried by a river.

Attrition is the wearing away of the load carried by a river. It creates smaller, rounder particles.

Hydraulic action is the force of air and water on the sides of rivers and in cracks.

Solution is the removal of chemical ions, especially calcium.

FACTORS AFFECTING EROSION

Load (the material carried by a river) - the heavier and sharper the load the greater the potential for erosion.

Velocity - the greater the velocity the greater the potential for erosion.

Gradient - increased gradient increases the rate of erosion.

Geology - soft, unconsolidated rocks such as sand and gravel are easily eroded.

pH - rates of solution are increased when the water is more acidic

Human impact - deforestation, dams and bridges interfere with the natural flow of a river and frequently end up increasing the rate of erosion.

TRANSPORT

Suspension - small particles are held up by turbulent flow in the river.

Saltation - heavier particles are bounced or bumped along the bed of the river.

Solution - the chemical load is carried dissolved in the water.

Traction - the heaviest material is dragged or rolled along the bed of the river.

Floatation - leaves and twigs are carried on the surface of the river.

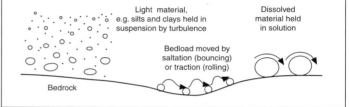

FEATURES OF EROSION

Waterfalls frequently occur on horizontally bedded rocks. The soft rock is undercut by hydraulic action and abrasion. The weight of the water and the lack of support cause the waterfall to collapse and retreat. Over thousands of years, the waterfall may retreat enough to form a gorge.

Ox-bow lakes are the result of erosion and deposition. Erosion is concentrated on the outer, deeper bank of a meander. During times of flooding, erosion increases. The river breaks through and creates a new, steeper channel. In time, the old meander is closed off by deposition to form an ox-bow lake.

Other features of erosion include pot holes, river cliffs, and V-shaped valleys.

WATERFALLS

1 Hydraulic impact
2 Abrasion of soft rock by hard fragments
3 Lack of support by soft rock
4 Weight of water causes unsupported hard rock to collapse

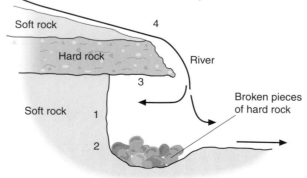

POT HOLES

Pot holes are formed by swirling water using boulders and stones to erode a small depression in the bed of a river.

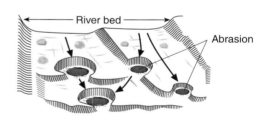

OX-BOW LAKES

1 Erosion (E) and deposition (D) around a meander (a bend in a river).
2 Increased erosion during flood conditions. The meander becomes exaggerated.
3 The river breaks through during a flood. Further deposition causes the old meander to become an ox-bow lake.

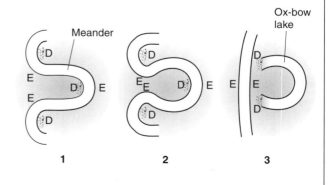

Deposition

Deposition occurs as a river slows down and it loses its energy. Typically, this occurs as a river floods across a flood plain, enters the sea or a dam. Features include deltas, levees, ox-bow lakes and flood plains.

FLOOD PLAIN

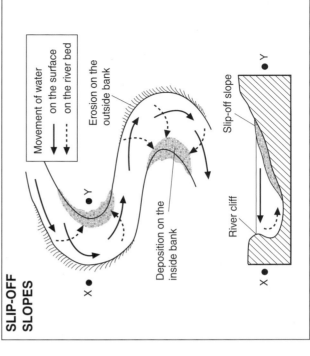

Levees

Flood plain

Line of bluffs

Ox-bow lake

Terrace

Sand and gravel

Silt and sand

Bedrock

SLIP-OFF SLOPES

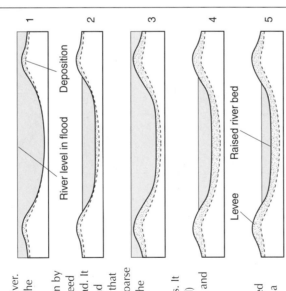

Movement of water
— on the surface
--- on the river bed

Erosion on the outside bank

Deposition on the inside bank

X ●

● Y

Slip-off slope

River cliff

X ●

● Y

LEVEES

Levees are raised banks at the edge of a river. They are formed by repeated flooding of the river. When the river floods, its speed is reduced. This is because it is slowed down by the vegetation on the floodplain. As its speed is reduced it has to deposit some of its load. It drops the coarser, heavier material first and the finer, lighter material last. This means that over centuries the levees are built up of coarse material, such as sand and gravel, while the flood plain consists of fine silt and clay.

1 When the river floods, it bursts its banks. It deposits its coarsest load (gravel and sand) closest to the bank and the finer load (silt and clay) further away.

2 3 4 This continues over a long time – centuries.

5 The river has built up raised banks called levees, consisting of coarse material, and a flood plain, consisting of fine material.

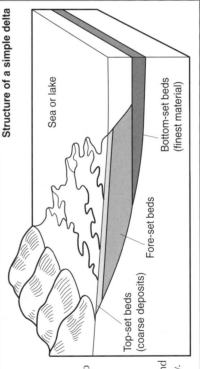

Deposition

River level in flood

Raised river bed

Levee

1
2
3
4
5

DELTAS

For deltas to be formed, a river needs to
• carry a large volume of sediment
• enter a still body of water.

Deposition is increased if the water is salty, as this causes salt particles to group together, become heavier and be deposited. Vegetation also increases the rate of deposition by slowing down the water.

The coarser material is deposited first, and the finest material last, and furthest away.

Structure of a simple delta

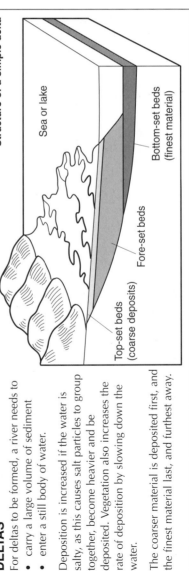

Sea or lake

Top-set beds (coarse deposits)

Fore-set beds

Bottom-set beds (finest material)

Rivers and human activity

Rivers are very attractive to people for a variety of reasons.
Rivers provide
- a source of drinking water
- fertile silt for agriculture
- a line of communication and navigation
- a source of power
- fishing
- recreation.

But rivers can also cause problems. The flood hazard is extremely dangerous for people's lives and their possessions. Many settlements are built on raised ground in order to reduce the risk of flooding. Oxford is an excellent example. Much of the flood plain of the Thames and the Cherwell has not been built upon. It has been left for farming and for recreational grounds. Housing and industry have tended to locate on the higher ground free from flooding.

People have also tried to reduce the effect of flooding by
- reinforcing river banks with steel, concrete, and wood
- diverting streams and creating new flood relief channels
- raising the banks of the river

Rivers are also affected by the building of dams. Dams
- reduce the speed of water flow
- control the amount of water in a river
- cause deposition behind the dam
- increase erosion below the dam ('clear water erosion')
- change ecosystems
- increase pressure on rocks and may cause earthquakes.

But they provide
- reliable water throughout the year
- navigation
- hydroelectric power
- water for irrigation
- safety from flooding.

The case study of the Three Gorges Dam on page 70 is an excellent example.

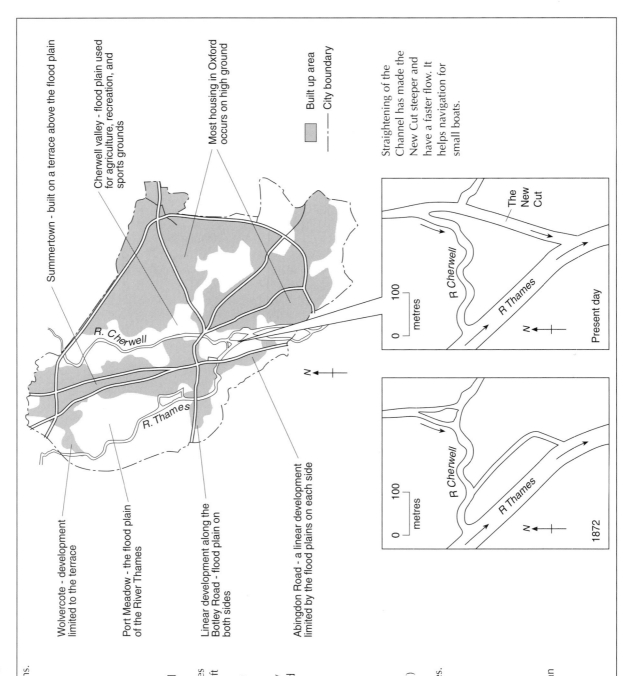

Summertown - built on a terrace above the flood plain

Cherwell valley - flood plain used for agriculture, recreation, and sports grounds

Most housing in Oxford occurs on high ground

Built up area

City boundary

Wolvercote - development limited to the terrace

Port Meadow - the flood plain of the River Thames

Linear development along the Botley Road - flood plain on both sides

Abingdon Road - a linear development limited by the flood plains on each side

R. Cherwell

R. Thames

N

Straightening of the Channel has made the New Cut steeper and have a faster flow. It helps navigation for small boats.

The New Cut

R Cherwell

R Thames

N

0   100
    metres

Present day

R Cherwell

R Thames

N

0   100
    metres

1872

Glaciation

GLACIAL SYSTEMS

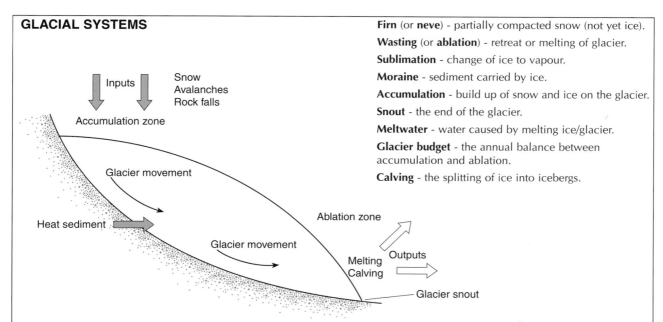

Firn (or **neve**) - partially compacted snow (not yet ice).

Wasting (or **ablation**) - retreat or melting of glacier.

Sublimation - change of ice to vapour.

Moraine - sediment carried by ice.

Accumulation - build up of snow and ice on the glacier.

Snout - the end of the glacier.

Meltwater - water caused by melting ice/glacier.

Glacier budget - the annual balance between accumulation and ablation.

Calving - the splitting of ice into icebergs.

A glacial system is the balance between inputs, storage, and outputs from a glacier. Inputs include accumulation of snow, avalanches, debris, heat, and meltwater. The main store is that of ice, but the glacier also carries debris, moraine, and meltwater. The outputs are the losses due to ablation, the melting of snow and ice, and sublimation of ice to vapour, as well as sediment.

The **regime** of the glacier refers to whether the glacier is advancing or retreating:

if accumulation > ablation the glacier advances
if accumulation < ablation the glacier retreats
if accumulation = ablation the glacier is steady.

HOW SNOW BECOMES ICE

Initially snow falls as flakes. With continued **accumulation** the lower snowflakes are compressed under more snow. They gradually change into ice pellets called **neve** or **firn**. Increased pressure causes the flakes to melt. With continued accumulation and pressure the neve becomes tightly packed. Any remaining air is expelled, its place is filled with freezing water. Thus, the neve changes into glacier ice, by compaction and crystallisation, with a characteristic bluish colour. The change from neve to ice occurs, typically, when the neve is 30m thick.

Glacial systems can be studied on an annual basis or on a much longer time scale. The size of a glacier depends on its regime i.e. the balance between the rate and amount of supply of ice and the amount and rate of ice loss. The glacier will have a **positive regime** when the supply is greater than loss by ablation (melting, evaporation, calving, wind erosion, avalanche etc.) and so the glacier will thicken and advance. A **negative regime** will occur when the wasting is greater than the supply (e.g. Rhone glacier today) thus the glacier will thin and retreat. Any glacier, though, can be divided into two sections, an area of accumulation at high altitudes generally, and an area of ablation at the snout.

GLACIAL BUDGETS: THE BALANCE BETWEEN ACCUMULATION AND ABLATION

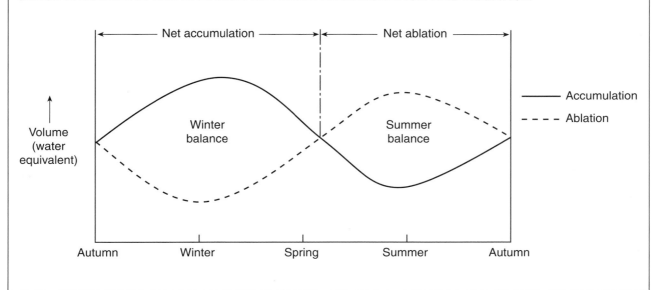

Glacial erosion

The amount and rate of erosion depends on
- the local geology
- the velocity of the glacier
- the weight and thickness of the ice
- the amount and character of the load carried.

The methods of glacial erosion include plucking and abrasion.

THE FORMATION OF A CIRQUE

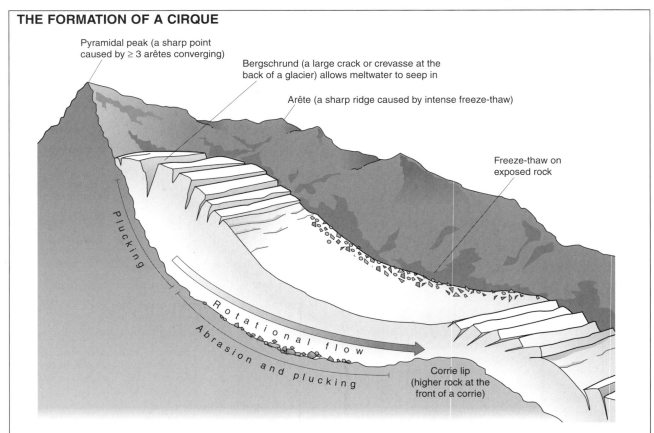

Pyramidal peak (a sharp point caused by ≥ 3 arêtes converging)

Bergschrund (a large crack or crevasse at the back of a glacier) allows meltwater to seep in

Arête (a sharp ridge caused by intense freeze-thaw)

Freeze-thaw on exposed rock

Plucking

Rotational flow

Abrasion and plucking

Corrie lip (higher rock at the front of a corrie)

PLUCKING
This occurs mostly at the base of the glacier and to an extent at the side. It is most effective in jointed rocks or those weakened by freeze-thaw. As the ice moves, meltwater seeps into the joints and freezes onto the rock, which is then ripped out by the moving glacier.

ABRASION
The debris carried by the glacier scrapes and scratches the rock leaving striations.

Other mechanisms include meltwater, freeze-thaw weathering, and pressure release. Although not strictly glacial nor erosional, these processes are crucial in the development of glacial scenery.

CIRQUES

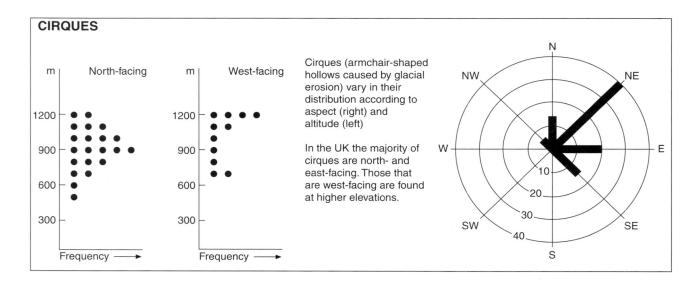

Cirques (armchair-shaped hollows caused by glacial erosion) vary in their distribution according to aspect (right) and altitude (left)

In the UK the majority of cirques are north- and east-facing. Those that are west-facing are found at higher elevations.

Landforms produced by glacial erosion

FEATURES OF GLACIAL EROSION

In the UK **cirques** are generally found on north- or east-facing slopes where accumulation is highest and ablation is lowest. They are formed after (**i**) a preglacial hollow is enlarged by freeze-thaw; (**ii**) ice accumulates in the hollow; (**iii**) having reached a critical weight and depth, the ice moves out in a rotational manner, eroding the floor by plucking and abrasion; (**iv**) meltwater trickles down the **bergschrund**, allowing the cirque to grow by freeze-thaw. After glaciation an armchair-shaped hollow remains, frequently filled with a lake, such as Red Tarn in the Lake District.

Other features of glacial erosion include **arêtes** and **pyramidal peaks** (horns) caused by the headward recession (cutting back) of two or more cirques. Glacial **troughs** (or U-shaped valleys) have steep sides and flat floors. In plan view they are straight since they have **truncated** the interlocking spurs of the preglacial valley. The ice may also carve deep **rock basins** frequently filled with **ribbon lakes**. **Hanging valleys** are formed by tributary glaciers which, unlike rivers, do not cut down to the level of the main valley, but are left suspended above. They are usually marked by waterfalls.

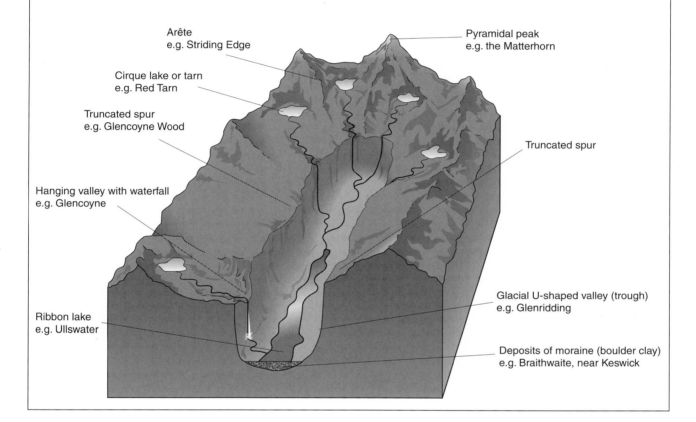

Arête
e.g. Striding Edge

Pyramidal peak
e.g. the Matterhorn

Cirque lake or tarn
e.g. Red Tarn

Truncated spur
e.g. Glencoyne Wood

Truncated spur

Hanging valley with waterfall
e.g. Glencoyne

Glacial U-shaped valley (trough)
e.g. Glenridding

Ribbon lake
e.g. Ullswater

Deposits of moraine (boulder clay)
e.g. Braithwaite, near Keswick

A **crag and tail** is formed when a very large resistant object obstructs ice flow. The ice is forced around the obstruction, eroding weaker rock. Material immediately in the lee of the obstruction is protected by the crag and forms a tail. Edinburgh Castle rock is an ancient volcanic plug, whereas its tail is formed of limestone.

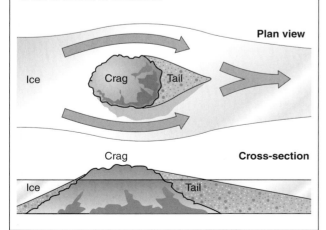

Plan view

Ice

Crag   Tail

Crag   Cross-section

Ice   Tail

Roches moutonnées vary in size from a few metres to hundreds of metres. They are smoothed and polished on the up valley side by abrasion but plucked on the lee side (down valley) as ice accelerates. They can be over 100m in height and several kilometres long.

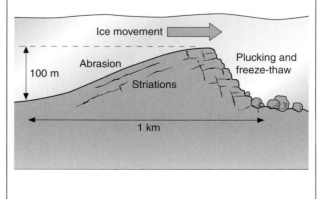

Ice movement

Abrasion   Plucking and freeze-thaw

100 m   Striations

1 km

Landforms produced by glacial deposition

Erratics are large boulders foreign to the local geology, e.g. the Bowder Stone in Borrowdale and the Norber Stone on the North Yorks Moors.

Moraines are lines of loose rocks, weathered from the valley sides and carried by the glaciers. At the snout of the glacier is a crescent shaped mound of **terminal moraine**. Its character is determined by the amount of load the glacier was carrying, the speed of movement and the rate of retreat. The finest example in Britain is the Cromer Ridge, up to 90m high and 8km wide.

Drumlins are small oval mounds up to 1.5km long and 100m high, e.g those in the Ribble Valley or the drowned drumlins of Clew Bay in Co. Mayo, Ireland. They are deposited due to friction between the ice and the underlying geology, causing the glacier to drop its load. As the glacier continues to advance it streamlines the mounds.

Many features can be used to determine the **direction of glacier movement**. Erratics pinpoint the origin of the material; drumlins and the long axes of pebbles in moraine are arranged in the direction of glacier movement.

Long axes of pebbles showing a NE–SW direction of movement

During glaciation

Pyramidal peak

Arête

Medial moraine

Lateral moraine

Ice

Terminal moraine

Subglacial moraine

Moraine

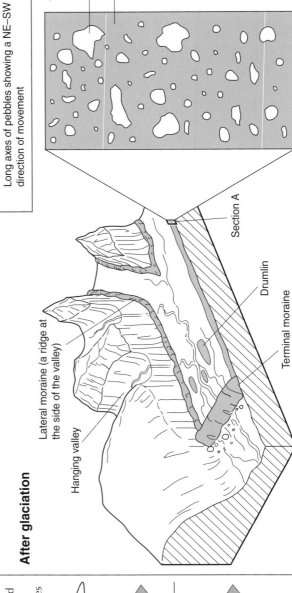

Section A enlarged

Boulders

Clay

5 metres

Angular unsorted

Section A

After glaciation

Lateral moraine (a ridge at the side of the valley)

Hanging valley

Drumlin

Terminal moraine

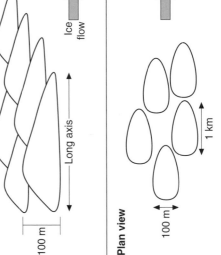

Long axis

100 m

Ice flow

Plan view

100 m

1 km

Meltwater landforms

Fluvioglacial or **meltwater** deposits are rounded and sorted. The most important ones are kames and eskers.

Eskers are elongated ridges of coarse, stratified, fluvioglacial sands and gravels. Two explanations are given for their formation: (**i**) material is deposited in subglacial meltwater tunnels or (**ii**) eskers may represent a rapidly retreating delta, formed as the ice melts and subglacial streams are suddenly released of pressure.

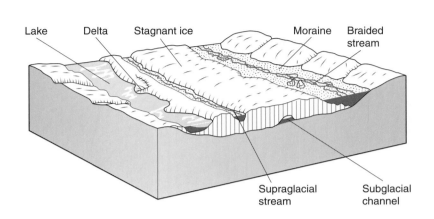

Lake Delta Stagnant ice Moraine Braided stream

Supraglacial stream Subglacial channel

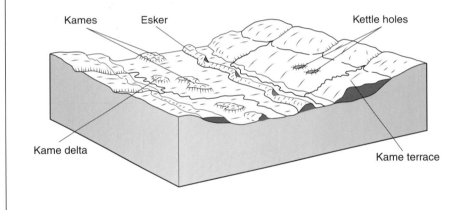

Kames Esker Kettle holes

Kame delta Kame terrace

Kames are irregular mounds of sorted sands and gravels, formed by supraglacial streams on stagnating ice sheets. Often they contain kettle holes, caused by the deposition of material around broken blocks of ice. **Kame terraces** are found at the side of the valley, laid down by streams occupying the site between the valley wall and the glacier, e.g. the Lammermuir Hills in eastern Scotland.

MELTWATER DEPOSITS

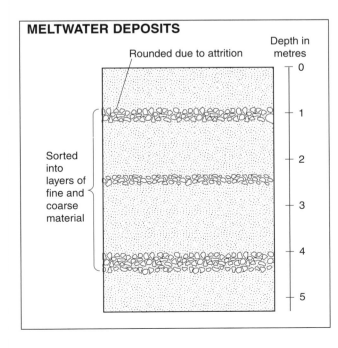

Rounded due to attrition

Depth in metres

Sorted into layers of fine and coarse material

0
1
2
3
4
5

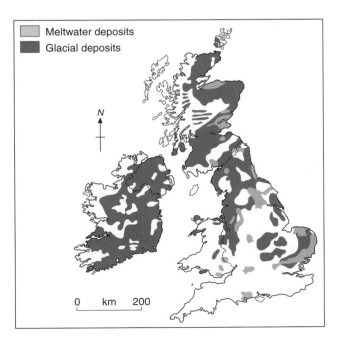

Meltwater deposits
Glacial deposits

N

0 km 200

Glacial landforms and human activity

Glacial landscapes provide many opportunities and constraints for human activity. In the **upland areas**, high rainfall, low temperatures, steep slopes, and thin soils make farming difficult. However, they are good for

- tourism, especially skiing and walking
- hydroelectric power and water supply
- forestry.

Lowland glacial areas often contain boulder clay. This is quite fertile soil, but it needs to be drained to avoid the risk of flooding. Kames and eskers are made from sand and gravel. These are used in the building industry. Sand and gravel is not very good for farming, because it is too acidic. Hence, many areas with sand and gravel have golf courses, quarries, and water parks in the flooded quarries.

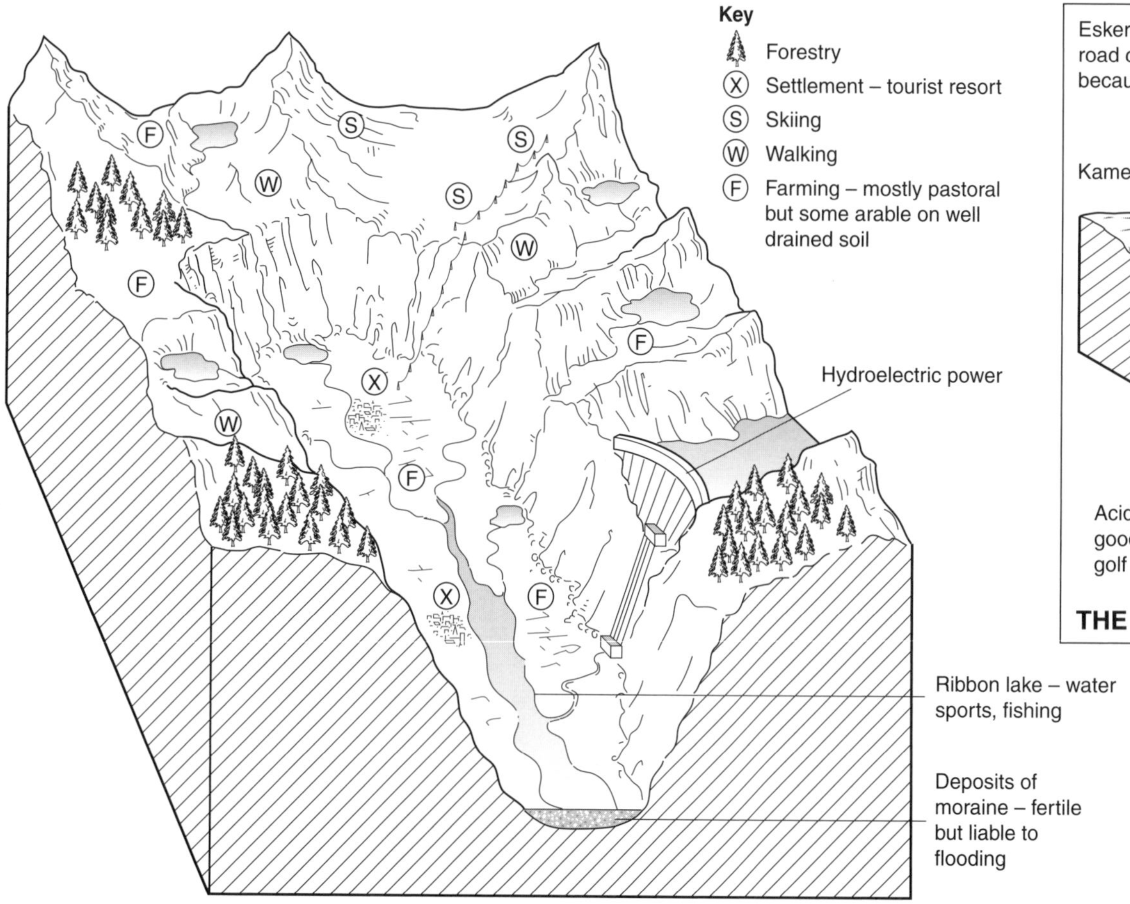

High ground – free from flooding – good for settlement

Kettle holes

Kame terrace

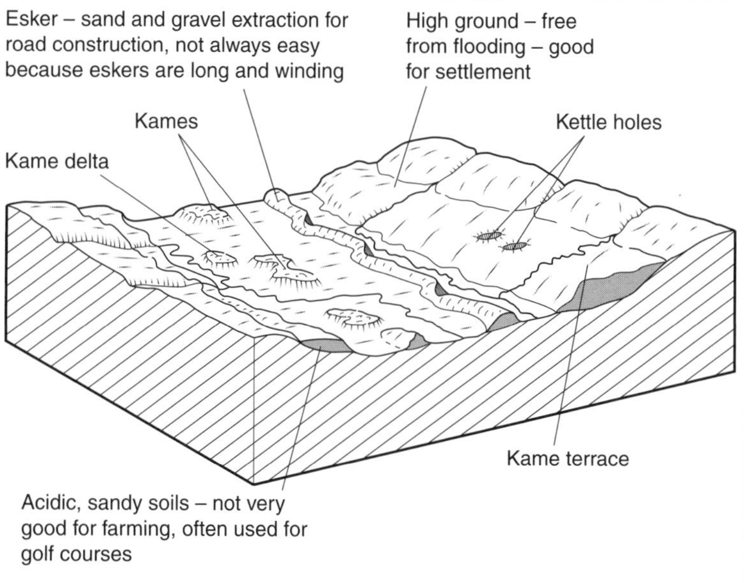

Esker – sand and gravel extraction for road construction, not always easy because eskers are long and winding

Kames

Kame delta

Acidic, sandy soils – not very good for farming, often used for golf courses

THE HUMAN USE OF GLACIAL LOWLANDS

Key
- 🌲 Forestry
- Ⓧ Settlement – tourist resort
- Ⓢ Skiing
- Ⓦ Walking
- Ⓕ Farming – mostly pastoral but some arable on well drained soil

Hydroelectric power

Ribbon lake – water sports, fishing

Deposits of moraine – fertile but liable to flooding

THE HUMAN USE OF GLACIAL HIGHLANDS

Managing coastal areas

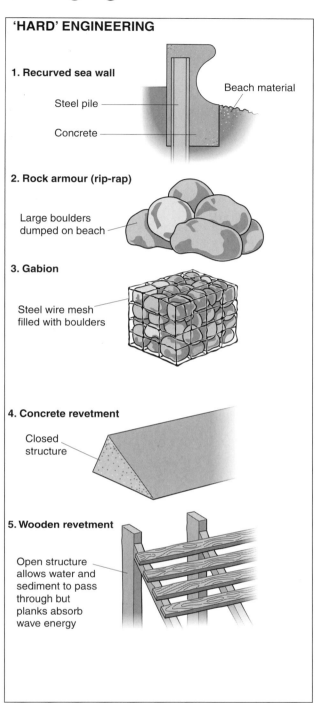

'HARD' ENGINEERING

1. Recurved sea wall

Steel pile

Concrete

Beach material

2. Rock armour (rip-rap)

Large boulders dumped on beach

3. Gabion

Steel wire mesh filled with boulders

4. Concrete revetment

Closed structure

5. Wooden revetment

Open structure allows water and sediment to pass through but planks absorb wave energy

THE PROBLEM WITH SEA WALLS

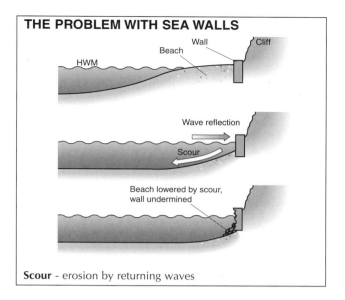

Wall
Cliff
Beach
HWM

Wave reflection

Scour

Beach lowered by scour, wall undermined

Scour - erosion by returning waves

MANAGED RETREAT

The cost of protecting Britain's coastline was up to £60 million annually until the early 1990s. Since then government cuts have reduced this. Part of the problem is that southern and eastern England are slowly sinking while sea level is rising. The risk of flooding and hence the cost of protection are rising. 'Managed retreat' allows nature to take its course: erosion in some areas, deposition in others. Benefits include less money spent and the creation of natural environments.

CASE STUDY: MANAGING THE FLOOD HAZARD AT CHISWELL

Chesil Beach is the main protection for Portland and Weymouth against the sea. Periodically, massive storms strike Chesil Beach and, on a number of occasions, storms have swept over the beach, flooding the village of Chiswell. In addition, water also percolates through the beach. **Percolation flooding** is the most regular type of flooding at Chiswell, although **overtopping** can be disastrous.

The sea defences which have been put in place as part of the flood alleviation scheme, comprise of metal cages called **gabions**, filled with pebbles from the Beach, and an **intercepting drain** which takes water coming over and through the Beach. The water is channelled away from housing and the road and into Portland Harbour. A **gabion mattress** on the top of the beach limits the amount of material moved from and over the top of the beach. In addition, housing and other developments in Chiswell have openings or **'opes'** between buildings to allow water to pass through.

During recent storm conditions, the flood alleviation scheme appears to have been successful in keeping flooding as a result of overtopping, to a minimum.

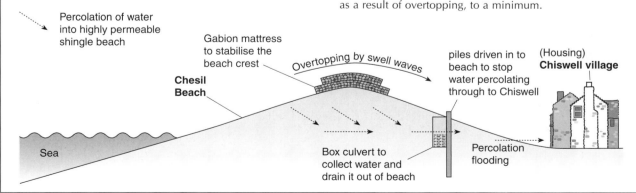

Percolation of water into highly permeable shingle beach

Gabion mattress to stabilise the beach crest

Chesil Beach

Overtopping by swell waves

piles driven in to beach to stop water percolating through to Chiswell

(Housing) **Chiswell village**

Sea

Box culvert to collect water and drain it out of beach

Percolation flooding

World climatic regions

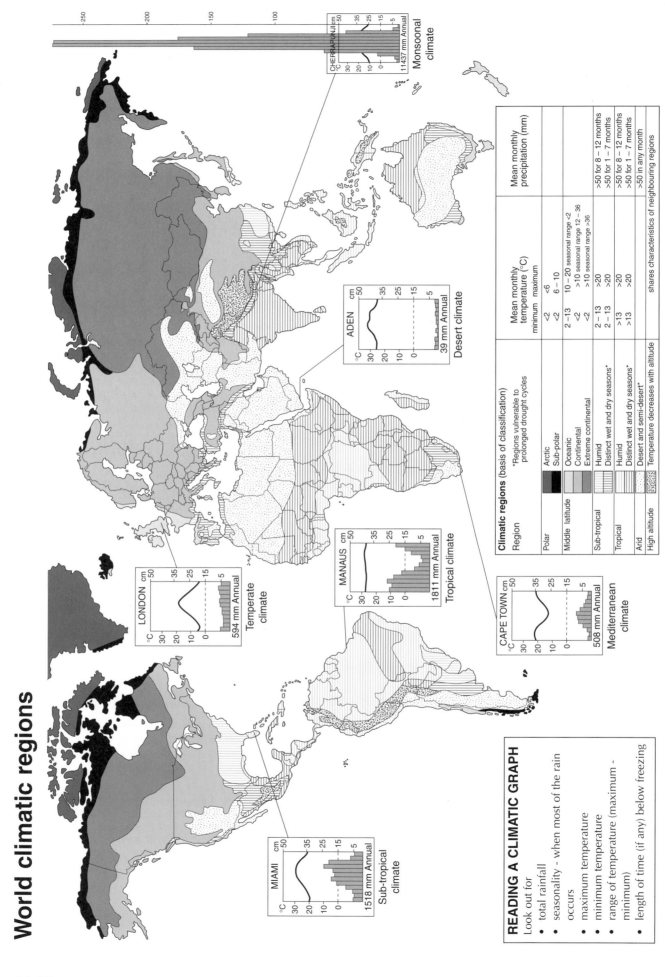

CHERRAPUNJI cm
°C
11437 mm Annual
Monsoonal climate

ADEN cm
°C
39 mm Annual
Desert climate

LONDON cm
°C
594 mm Annual
Temperate climate

MANAUS cm
°C
1811 mm Annual
Tropical climate

CAPE TOWN cm
°C
508 mm Annual
Mediterranean climate

MIAMI cm
°C
1518 mm Annual
Sub-tropical climate

Climatic regions (basis of classification)

*Regions vulnerable to prolonged drought cycles

Region		Mean monthly temperature (°C) minimum maximum	Mean monthly precipitation (mm)
Polar	Arctic	<2 <6	
	Sub-polar	<2 6 – 10	
Middle latitude	Oceanic	10 – 20 seasonal range <2	
	Continental	<2 >10 seasonal range 12 – 36	
	Extreme continental	<2 >10 seasonal range >36	
Sub-tropical	Humid	2 – 13 >20	>50 for 8 – 12 months
	Distinct wet and dry seasons*	2 – 13 >20	>50 for 1 – 7 months
Tropical	Humid	>13 >20	>50 for 8 – 12 months
	Distinct wet and dry seasons*	>13 >20	>50 for 1 – 7 months
Arid	Desert and semi-desert*		>50 in any month
High altitude	Temperature decreases with altitude		shares characteristics of neighbouring regions

READING A CLIMATIC GRAPH

Look out for

- total rainfall
- seasonality - when most of the rain occurs
- maximum temperature
- minimum temperature
- range of temperature (maximum - minimum)
- length of time (if any) below freezing

Factors affecting temperature

LATITUDE

Areas that are close to the Equator receive more heat than areas that are close to the Poles. This is due to two reasons:

1 incoming solar radiation (insolation) is concentrated near the Equator, but dispersed near the Poles

2 insolation near the Poles has to pass through a greater amount of atmosphere and there is more chance of it being reflected back out to space.

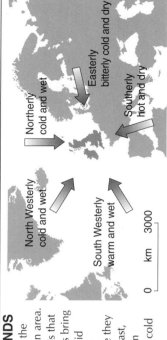

Near the Poles insolation has more atmosphere to pass through

Solar radiation (insolation)

Atmosphere

At the Equator insolation is concentrated, but near the Poles it is dispersed over a wider area

DISTANCE FROM THE SEA

It takes more energy to heat up water than it does to heat land. However, it takes longer for water to lose heat. Hence, land is hotter than the sea by day, but colder than the sea by night. Places that are close to the sea are cool by day, but mild by night. With increasing distance from the sea this effect is reduced.

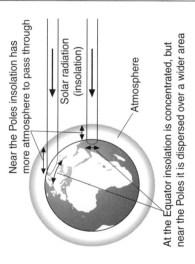

Summer   Incoming heat from the Sun

15°C (warm)
Coastal region cooled by sea air

10°C (cool)
Land absorbs heat quickly

Sea absorbs heat slowly

Winter   Out going heat from the earth

0°C (cold)
Coastal region warmed by sea air

5°C (cool)
Land loses heat rapidly

Sea loses heat slowly

ASPECT

Aspect is the direction a place faces. On a local scale aspect is very important. In the British Isles south facing places are warmer than north and east facing places.

Sun

Sunny (adret)
South slope – south facing

Shady (ubac)
North slope – north facing

HILL

South slope – north facing

North slope – south facing

VALLEY

South   **North**

PREVAILING WINDS

Prevailing winds are the dominant winds in an area. The south west winds that affect the British Isles bring warm air from the mid Atlantic. Their effect depends upon where they come from. By contrast, north east winds from Siberia bring bitterly cold conditions in winter.

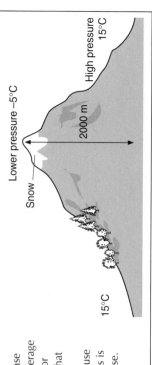

Northerly cold and wet

Easterly bitterly cold and dry

North Westerly cold and wet

Southerly hot and dry

South Westerly warm and wet

0   km   3000

ALTITUDE

Temperatures decrease with altitude. On average it drops about 1°C for every 100 metres. That means 10°C over 1000m. This is because air at higher altitudes is thinner and less dense.

High pressure
15°C

Lower pressure –5°C

2000 m

Snow

15°C

OCEAN CURRENTS

The effect of an ocean current depends upon whether it is a warm current or a cold one. Warm currents move away from the Equator, whereas cold currents move towards it. The cold Labrador Current reduces the temperatures of the western side of the Atlantic, while the warm North Atlantic Drift raises temperatures on the eastern side.

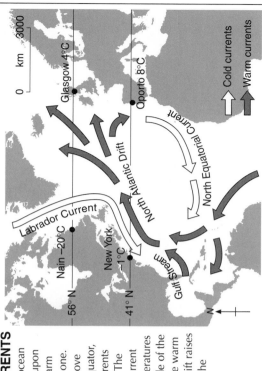

Glasgow 4°C

Oporto 8°C

North Equatorial Current

North Atlantic Drift

Labrador Current

Nain –20°C

New York –1°C

Gulf Stream

56° N

41° N

0   km   3000

Cold currents

Warm currents

N

Types of rainfall

CONVECTIONAL

When the land becomes very hot it heats the air above it. This air expands and rises. As it rises cooling and condensation take place. If it continues to rise rain will fall. It is very common in tropical areas. In Britain it is quite common in the summer, especially in the South East.

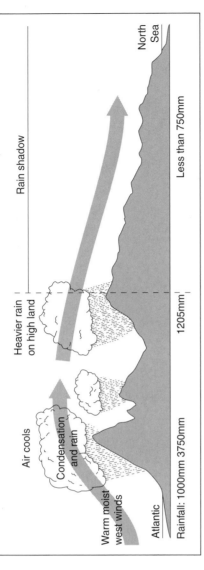

3 Further ascent causes more expansion and more cooling; rain takes place

Cumulus cloud

3

Rising warm air 2

4 Cool air descends and replaces the warm air

2 The heated air rises, expands and cools; condensation takes place

Ground level

Rain

1 The earth's hot surface heats the air above it

FRONTAL OR CYCLONIC

Frontal rain occurs when warm air meets cold air. The warm air, being lighter and less dense, is forced to rise over the cold, denser air. As it rises it cools, condenses and forms rain.

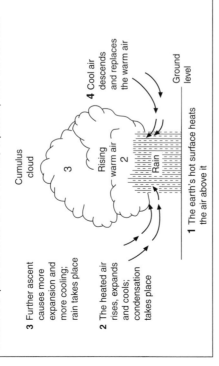

Warm air rises over cold air; it expands, cools and condensation takes place; clouds and rain form

Warm air

Cumulus cloud

Rain

This line represents the plane separating warm air from cold air

Cold air

Warm air is forced to rise when it is undercut by colder air; clouds and rain occur

RELIEF OR OROGRAPHIC

Air may be forced to rise over a barrier such as a mountain. As it rises it cools, condenses and forms rain. There is often a rain shadow effect whereby the leeward (downwind) slope receives a relatively small amount of rain.

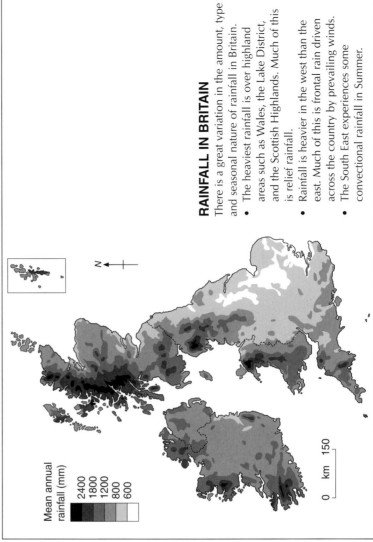

Air cools

Heavier rain on high land

Rain shadow

North Sea

Cumulus cloud

Condensation and rain

Warm moist west winds

Atlantic

Rainfall: 1000mm 3750mm

1205mm

Less than 750mm

RAINFALL IN BRITAIN

There is a great variation in the amount, type and seasonal nature of rainfall in Britain.

- The heaviest rainfall is over highland areas such as Wales, the Lake District, and the Scottish Highlands. Much of this is relief rainfall.
- Rainfall is heavier in the west than the east. Much of this is frontal rain driven across the country by prevailing winds.
- The South East experiences some convectional rainfall in Summer.

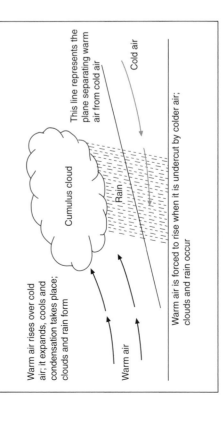

N

Mean annual rainfall (mm)

2400
1800
1200
800
600

0 km 150

The greenhouse effect

The greenhouse effect is the term given to global warming. The earth's atmosphere acts like a greenhouse. It allows short-wave ultra-violet radiation in but it stops long wave infra-red radiation from escaping. So, over time, the atmosphere heats up.

Greenhouse gases include
- carbon dioxide released by the burning of fossil fuels
- methane produced by livestock
- CFCs (chloroflourocarbons) from aerosols.

Global warming has good and bad results.
In Canada, for example, it will lead to
- bigger crop yields
- a longer growing season
- a longer tourist season
- less skiing
- more drought
- a decline in the forestry industry.

THE GREENHOUSE EFFECT

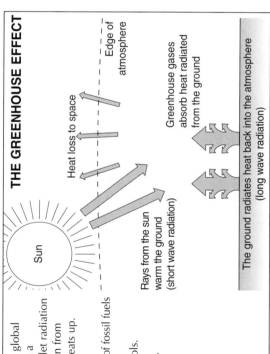

Sun

Heat loss to space

Edge of atmosphere

Rays from the sun warm the ground (short wave radiation)

Greenhouse gases absorb heat radiated from the ground

The ground radiates heat back into the atmosphere (long wave radiation)

FLOODING IN BANGLADESH

Rising sea levels
one of the most important changes will be the rise in sea level. this will have a great impact on low lying areas such as Bangladesh.

Inlets and estuaries
- will be enlarged and deepened
- salt levels will increase, affecting agriculture

Low lying areas
- will be permanently flooded
- loss of fertile agricultural land

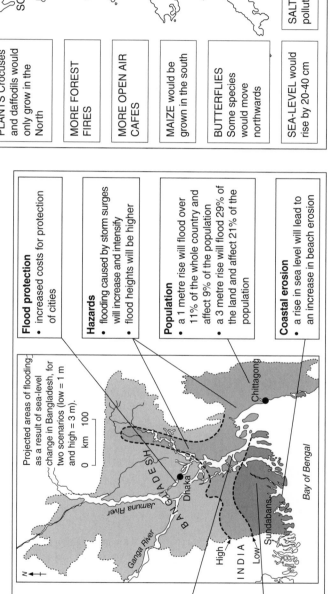

Projected areas of flooding as a result of sea-level change in Bangladesh, for two scenarios (low = 1 m and high = 3 m).

0   km   100

BANGLADESH

Ganga River
Jamuna River
Dhaka
High
Low
Sundabans
INDIA
Chittagong
Bay of Bengal

Flood protection
- increased costs for protection of cities

Hazards
- flooding caused by storm surges will increase and intensify
- flood heights will be higher

Population
- a 1 metre rise will flood over 11% of the whole country and affect 9% of the population
- a 3 metre rise will flood 29% of the land and affect 21% of the population

Coastal erosion
- a rise in sea level will lead to an increase in beach erosion

---

THE POTENTIAL IMPACT OF THE GREENHOUSE EFFECT ON BRITAIN

BIRDS Arctic species, such as Capercaillie, Ptarmigan, Snow Bunting and Dotterel would face extinction

SKIING Little or no snow would force Aviemore to close down

FLOODING Defences would need to be provided or rebuilt in low areas.
AT RISK: East Anglia
Kent
Lincolnshire
Thames Estuary
Solway Firth
Ribble Estuary

WETLANDS and inland marshes would dry up. Birds such as Greenshank & Dunlin would be under threat

TEMPERATURE would rise by 1.5-4.5°C

TREES Deciduous trees would replace conifers

INSECTS Swarms would occur

VINES would flourish

PLANTS Crocuses and daffodils would only grow in the North

MORE FOREST FIRES

MORE OPEN AIR CAFES

MAIZE would be grown in the south

BUTTERFLIES Some species would move northwards

SEA-LEVEL would rise by 20-40 cm

SALT WATER would pollute freshwater

N

LINCOLNSHIRE
EAST ANGLIA
THAMES
KENT
SOLWAY
RIBBLE

At risk

0   km   150

Climate 29

Soils

Soils form the outer-most part of the earth's surface, and are made up of weathered rock, organic matter, air, and water. Soil has material in all three states - solid, liquid, and gas.

SOIL TEXTURE

Soil texture refers to the size of the soil particles. Soil texture is very important. It affects
- the moisture content and aeration of the soil
- retention of nutrients
- ease of cultivation and root penetration.

In general, clay soils become waterlogged, whereas sandy soils drain very rapidly. A loam (mixed) soil is best.

Particle size	Diameter (mm)
Clay	< 0.002
Silt	< 0.02
Sand	< 0.2
Gravel	≥ 0.2

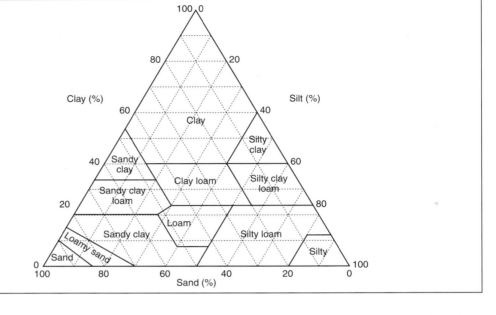

SOIL STRUCTURE

The shape of the individual soil particles is known as soil structure.

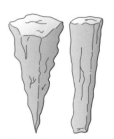

Blocky 5-75mm   Columnar 10-100mm   Crumb 1-6mm   Platy 1-10mm   Prismatic 10-100mm

SOIL HORIZONS

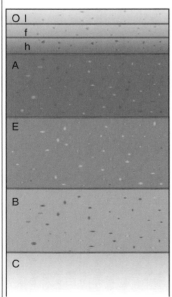

O Organic horizon
l   Undecomposed litter (plant remains)
f   partly decomposed (fermenting) litter
h   well decomposed humus (decayed plant remains)

A Mixed mineral-organic horizon
h   humus
p   ploughed, as in a field or a garden
g   gleyed or waterlogged

E Eluvial or leached horizon
a   strongly leached, ash coloured horizon, as in a podzol
b   weakly leached, light brown horizon, as in a brown earth

B Illuvial or deposited horizon
fe iron deposited
t   clay deposited
h   humus deposited

C Bedrock or parent material

Soil horizons are the layers within a soil. They vary in terms of texture, structure, colour, pH, and mineral content. The top layer of vegetation is referred to as the Organic (O) horizon. Beneath this is the mixed mineral-organic layer (A horizon). It is generally a dark colour due to the presence of organic matter. An Ap horizon is one that has been mixed by ploughing.

In some soils leaching (removal) takes place. This removes material from the E horizon. Consequently, the layer is much lighter in colour. In a podzol, where leaching is intense, an ash-coloured Ea horizon is formed. By contrast, in a brown earth, where leaching is less intense, a light brown Eb horizon is found.

The B horizon is the deposited or illuvial horizon. This contains material that has been moved from the E horizon, such as iron (fe) humus (h) and clay (t).

At the base of the horizon is the parent material or bedrock.

Soil formation

CLIMATE AND MAJOR SOIL TYPES

Two important mechanisms exist:
- precipitation effectiveness
- temperature

Precipitation effectiveness is a measure of how far precipitation (Ppt) exceeds potential evapotranspiration (P.Evt).
- If Ppt > P.Evt there is a downward movement of materials in the soil, and the soil is leached.
- If Ppt < P.Evt there is an upward movement of material.

Temperature affects the rate of biological and chemical action. In general, as temperatures increase so too does chemical and biological activity.

Wet / Dry / Cold / Hot

Cold (ice) desert soils
Tundra soils
Podzols
Brown earths
Chernozems
Chestnuts
Hot desert soils
Ferruginous soils

TIME

Time is not a causative factor, but allows processes to operate. The time needed for soil formation varies. Sandstones develop soils more quickly than granite or basalt. Some British soils have evolved since the last glaciation. Soils which have not had enough time to properly mature are termed **azonal** soils.

PLANTS AND ANIMALS

The effects of plants and animals include micro-organisms breaking down leaf litter, worms mixing soils, vegetation returning nutrients, and human activities such as adding fertiliser, irrigating, draining, and compacting soils.

Soil formation is affected by a number of factors, notably climate, geology, biological organisms, and topography. These interact over time to produce distinctive soils and soil profiles.

GEOLOGY

Geology has a lasting effect on soils through texture, structure, and fertility. Sandstones produce free, draining soils, whereas clays give much finer soils. On a regional scale, soils often vary with geology, as in the case of the Isle of Purbeck.

The **intrazonal** classification states that within a climatic zone soils vary with rock types.

Rock type	Soil type
Sands and gravel	Podzols
Chalk	Rendzina
Clay	Brown earths and gleys
Limestone	Rendzina

Isle of Purbeck

RELIEF

- Steeper slopes have thinner soils.
- Soil erosion increases with slope angle.
- Aspect affects micro-climate (small-scale variations in climate).
- A **catena** is the variation in soils along a slope owing to changes in slope angle and drainage, climate, and water table. Rock type is constant.

Altitude	1000 m	
Rainfall	1000 mm	
Average temperature	7°C	

Altitude	250 m	
Rainfall	750 mm	
Average temperature	11°C	

Surface water gley
Podzol
Brown earth
Peaty brown earth
Groundwater gley
Water table
Soil type

Soil processes

Humification, degradation, and mineralisation are the processes whereby organic matter is broken down and the nutrients are returned to the soil. The break down releases organic acids which break down clay to silica, and soluble iron and aluminium.

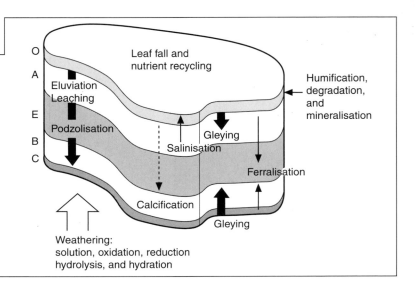

PODZOLISATION

- An intense form of leaching involving the removal of minerals under acidic conditions.
- A pH of less than 4.5 dissolves minerals such as silica, iron (Fe), aluminium (Al).
- Deposition of humus, iron, and aluminium occurs in the B horizon while other nutrients are leached out of the soil.
- Rapid snow melt increases leaching.

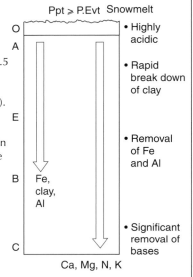

FERRALISATION

In tropical areas, under hot, wet conditions, vegetation is broken down rapidly - hence the A and O horizons do not become acidic. Leaching is rapid - but under low levels of acidity, iron and aluminium remain in the soil. Hence, the soil has a typical red colour, indicating the presence of iron.

LEACHING

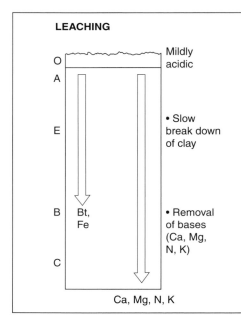

Leaching is the removal of material from the upper part to the lower part of the soil.

Illuviation is the deposition of material in the lower part of the soil.

Calcification results from ineffective leaching, in areas of low rainfall, causing the accumulation of calcium in the soil.

Salinisation is the upward movement of soluble salts by capillary action (water drawn up to an evaporating surface and up by plants), and their deposition in the surface horizons, forming a toxic crust.

CALCIFICATION

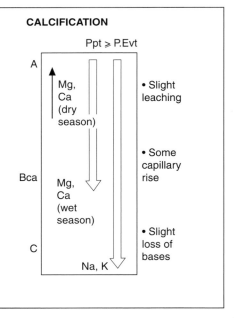

Soil types

SOIL TYPES AND MAJOR PROCESSES

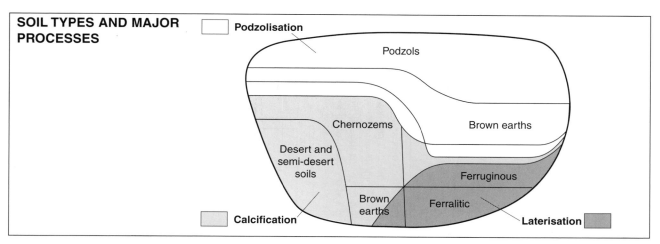

Podzolisation

Podzols

Chernozems

Brown earths

Desert and semi-desert soils

Ferruginous

Brown earths

Ferralitic

Calcification

Laterisation

Podzols

Coniferous/heathland vegetation, mor humus, pH 4.5 or less

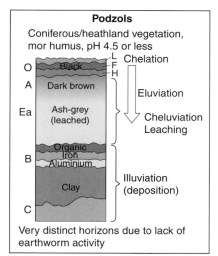

Very distinct horizons due to lack of earthworm activity

Brown earth

Deciduous vegetation, mull humus, mildly acidic, pH 5.5-6.5

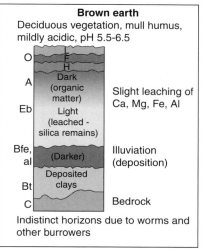

Indistinct horizons due to worms and other burrowers

Chernozem

Grassland vegetation, Ppt = P.Evt

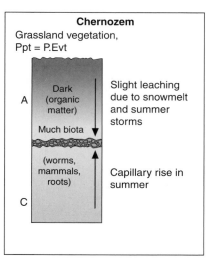

Ferralitic (latosol)

Tropical rainforest, Ppt > P.Evt

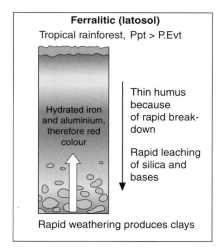

Rapid weathering produces clays

Groundwater gley

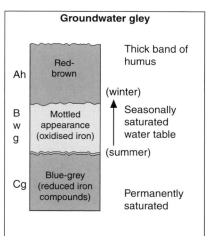

Rendzina

Grass vegetation

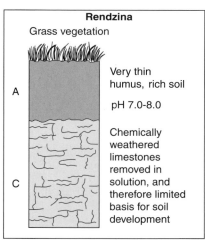

Surface water gley

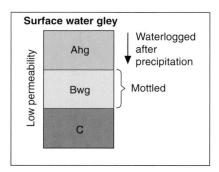

Ferruginous soil

Savanna vegetation, distinct wet and dry seasons

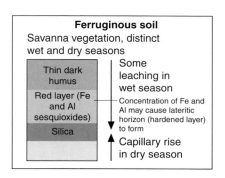

Human impact on soils

SOIL EROSION

Soil erosion in North America: the effect of land use

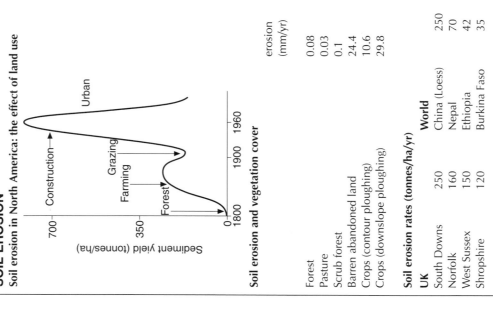

Soil erosion and vegetation cover

	erosion (mm/yr)
Forest	0.08
Pasture	0.03
Scrub forest	0.1
Barren abandoned land	24.4
Crops (contour ploughing)	10.6
Crops (downslope ploughing)	29.8

Soil erosion rates (tonnes/ha/yr)

UK		World	
South Downs	250	China (Loess)	250
Norfolk	160	Nepal	70
West Sussex	150	Ethiopia	42
Shropshire	120	Burkina Faso	35

SALINISATION

This occurs when excessive irrigation water causes the water table (water level in rocks) to rise to the surface. As the water evaporates, soluble salts are left forming a toxic saline crust.

SOIL COMPACTION

A change in structure from a free draining soil to a compact, impermeable horizon. **A plough pan** forms when damp soil is ploughed and moulded. Compaction by the weight of machinery increases the problem.

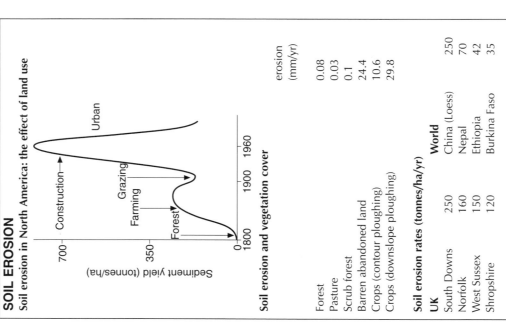

PRINCIPLES OF GOOD SOIL MANAGEMENT

- Soil reclamation (drainage e.g. Fens & Polders, build-up of humus)
- Runoff control (contour ploughing, humus application)
- Crop management (rotation, cover crops)
- Erosion control (diguettes, check dams)
- Revegetation (afforestation)

STAGES IN FOOT PATH EROSION

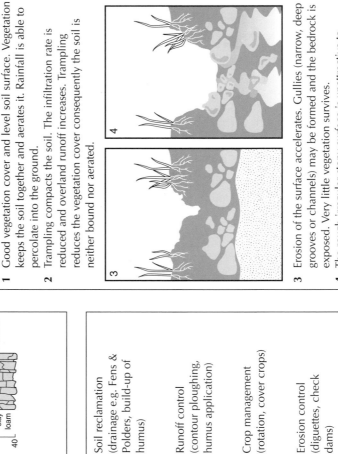

1 Good vegetation cover and level soil surface. Vegetation keeps the soil together and aerates it. Rainfall is able to percolate into the ground.

2 Trampling compacts the soil. The infiltration rate is reduced and overland runoff increases. Trampling reduces the vegetation cover consequently the soil is neither bound nor aerated.

3 Erosion of the surface accelerates. Gullies (narrow, deep grooves or channels) may be formed and the bedrock is exposed. Very little vegetation survives.

4 The rough irregular stony surface is unattractive to walkers and may even be dangerous. As a result walkers begin to use the vegetated areas at the side of the footpath and the process begins again.

Ecosystems

An **ecosystem** is the interaction of plants and animals with their living and non-living environments. **Biogeography** is the geographic distribution of soils, vegetation and ecosystems - where they are and why they are there.

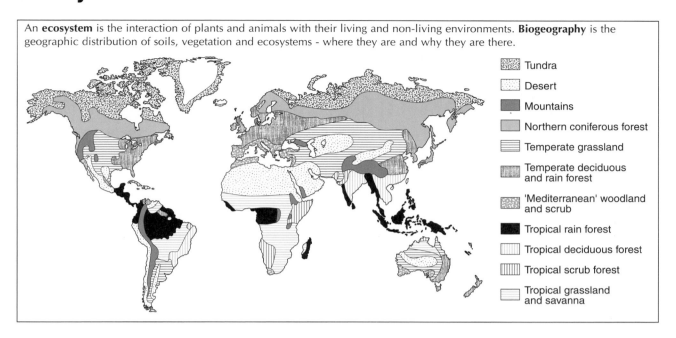

- Tundra
- Desert
- Mountains
- Northern coniferous forest
- Temperate grassland
- Temperate deciduous and rain forest
- 'Mediterranean' woodland and scrub
- Tropical rain forest
- Tropical deciduous forest
- Tropical scrub forest
- Tropical grassland and savanna

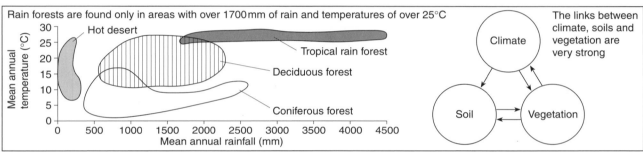

Rain forests are found only in areas with over 1700mm of rain and temperatures of over 25°C

The links between climate, soils and vegetation are very strong

Ecosystems can be divided into two main components:
- **Abiotic** elements (non-living), e.g. air, water, heat, nutrients, rock, and sediments
- **Biotic** elements (living), e.g. plants and animals. These can be divided into

1 **Autotrophs** (or producers) - organisms capable of converting sunlit energy into food energy by photosynthesis
2 **Heterotrophs** (or consumers) - organisms that must feed on other organisms, e.g.

   herbivores - plant eaters
   carnivores - meat eaters
   omnivores - plant and meat eaters
   detritivores - decomposers

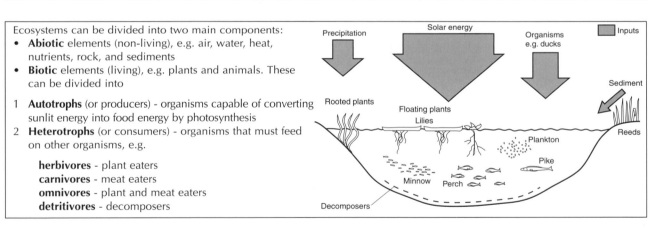

THE TROPHIC PYRAMID

The trophic pyramid shows us that there are a large number of producers, which are mostly plants, and a smaller number of herbivores, and an even smaller number of carnivores.

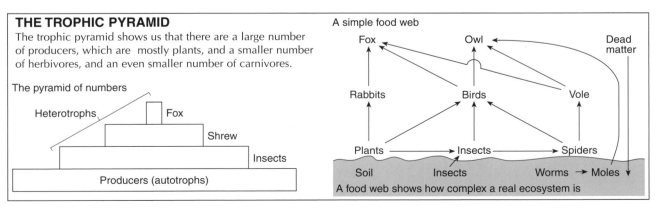

A simple food web

A food web shows how complex a real ecosystem is

Tropical rain forests

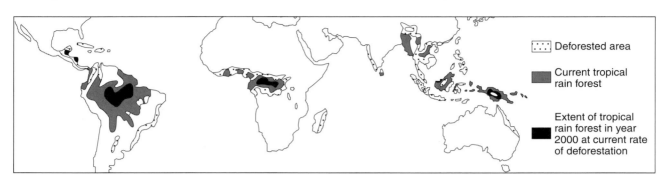

⠿	Deforested area
▨	Current tropical rain forest
■	Extent of tropical rain forest in year 2000 at current rate of deforestation

CLIMATE

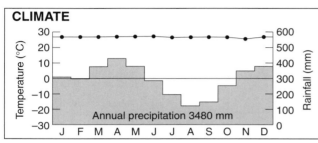

Annual precipitation 3480 mm

Some features of a rain forest climate:

- Annual temperatures are high (26-27°C), owing to the equatorial location of rain forest areas.
- Seasonal ranges are low, 1-2°C, and diurnal ranges (daily) are greater, 10-15°C.
- Rainfall is high (> 2000mm), intense, convectional, and occurs on about 250 days each year.
- Humidity levels on the ground are high, often 100%.
- The growing season is year round.

VEGETATION

- The vegetation is evergreen, enabling photosynthesis to take place year round.
- It is layered, and the shape of the crowns vary with the layer, in order to receive light.
- Rain forests are very productive ecosystems.
- The ecosystem is diverse: up to 200 species of tree per ha (an area the size of a rugby pitch) and include figs, teak, mahogany, and yellow woods.

A
Wide-spaced umbrella-shaped crowns, straight trunks, and high branches

B
Medium-spaced mop-shaped crowns

C
Densely-packed conical-shaped crowns

D
Sparse vegetation of shrubs and saplings

F Root layers

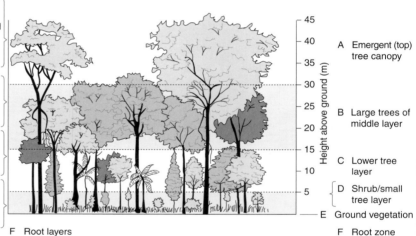

A Emergent (top) tree canopy

B Large trees of middle layer

C Lower tree layer

D Shrub/small tree layer

E Ground vegetation

F Root zone

SOILS

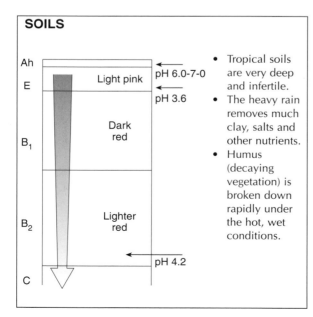

- Tropical soils are very deep and infertile.
- The heavy rain removes much clay, salts and other nutrients.
- Humus (decaying vegetation) is broken down rapidly under the hot, wet conditions.

Main conflicts:

Cattle ranching	South America
Banana plantations	Costa Rica, South America
Coffee plantations	Africa
Logging	All over
Farming	All over
Mining	South America, Asia, Africa
Rubber plantations	Indonesia

DESTRUCTION OF THE TROPICAL RAIN FOREST

- Annual loss of rain forest is 40 million acres, the size of England and Wales:

Latin America	20.5 million acres
Africa	11.0 million
Asia	9.0 million

- Disappearing at an acre per second
- Rain forests support up to 90% of all wildlife
- Annual deforestation in the 1990s was 50% higher than in the 1980s
- Over 200 million people live in the rain forest

Shifting cultivation and rain forest soils

In many tropical rain forests shifting cultivation is the main type of farming. This involves clearing a plot of land, and cultivating it for a few years. When the soil fertility has dropped and farming can no longer continue, they move to another plot.

Until recently, many geographers believed that rain forest soils regained their fertility quickly - about twenty years or so after being used for farming (a). Now it is realised that fertility does not recover and continued use of the rain forest leads to a long term decline in soil fertility (b).

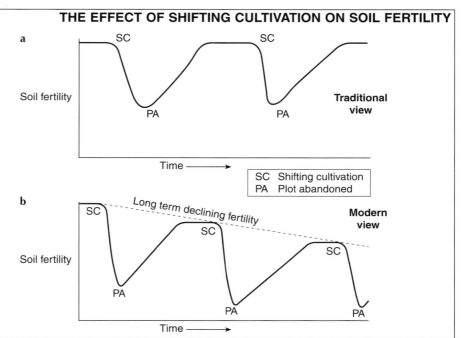

THE EFFECT OF SHIFTING CULTIVATION ON SOIL FERTILITY

a

Soil fertility

SC   SC

PA   PA

Traditional view

Time ——→

SC   Shifting cultivation
PA   Plot abandoned

b

Soil fertility

Long term declining fertility

SC

SC

SC

PA   PA   PA

Modern view

Time ——→

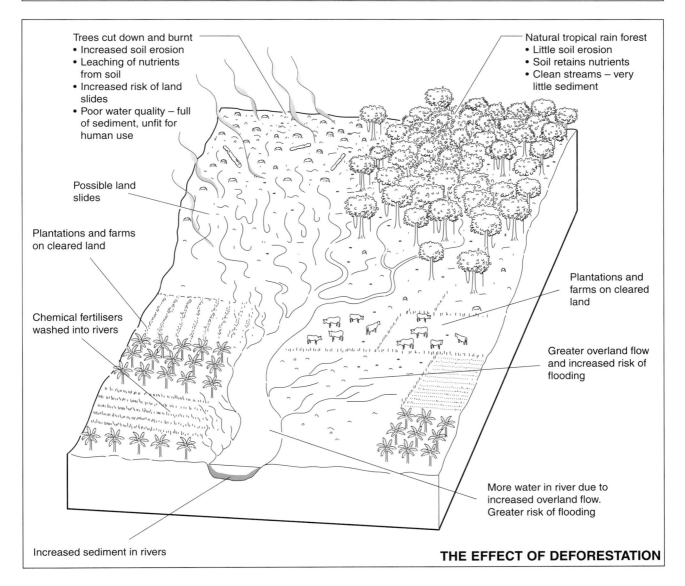

Trees cut down and burnt
• Increased soil erosion
• Leaching of nutrients from soil
• Increased risk of land slides
• Poor water quality – full of sediment, unfit for human use

Possible land slides

Plantations and farms on cleared land

Chemical fertilisers washed into rivers

Increased sediment in rivers

Natural tropical rain forest
• Little soil erosion
• Soil retains nutrients
• Clean streams – very little sediment

Plantations and farms on cleared land

Greater overland flow and increased risk of flooding

More water in river due to increased overland flow. Greater risk of flooding

THE EFFECT OF DEFORESTATION

Deciduous woodland

WORLD DISTRIBUTION

There are no large scale outcrops of deciduous forest in the southern hemisphere, due to the absence of land at an appropriate latitude.

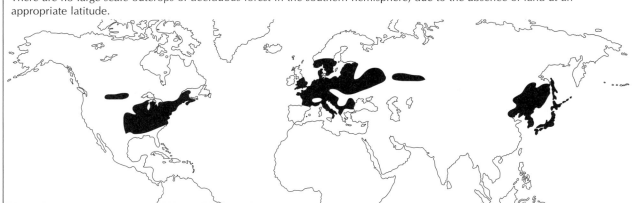

CLIMATE

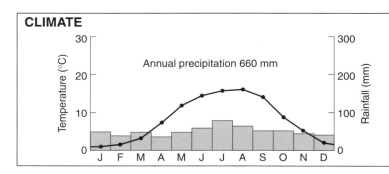

- There are wide variations in the climate, e.g. between North-East USA and South-West Ireland.
- Rainfall is 1000-1500 mm; it is mostly frontal rainfall, and in Winter.
- Winters below freezing for 2-3 months in eastern China and North-East USA, but mild in western Europe due to the North Atlantic Drift.
- Cool summers 15-20°C.

SOIL

- Soils are generally quite fertile brown earths.
- The humus is mildly acidic.
- Soil fauna, such as earthworms, flourish mixing the layers and all the nutrients.
- Decomposition of leaves takes up to 9 months.

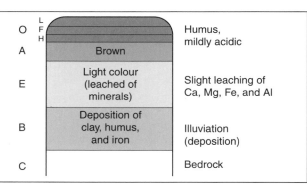

VEGETATION

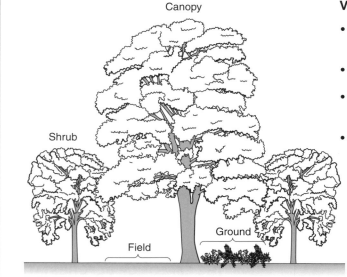

- Deciduous trees shed their leaves in winter to retain moisture, conserve nutrients, and avoid damage by snow/ice.
- The ecosystem is very productive due to high summer temperatures and the long day length.
- Vegetation varies with soil type. Birch and rowan are found on acid soils, whereas box and maple occur on alkaline soils. Oak can tolerate either type of soil.
- Shrub vegetation varies with light. Some need light and flower early, such as the wood anemone. Others can tolerate dark such as dog's mercury and ivy.

Coniferous (boreal) forests

WORLD DISTRIBUTION

There are no large scale outcrops of boreal forest in the southern hemisphere, due to the absence of land at an appropriate latitude.

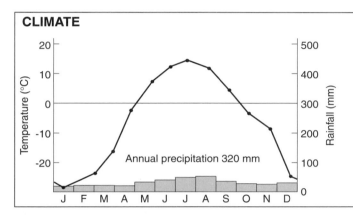

CLIMATE

- Rainfall is low, (<500 mm per year), with no real seasonal pattern. Snowfall is frequent in winter, and frosts occur in summer.
- Summer temperatures 10-15°C, with winter temperatures below freezing for up to 6 months.
- Growing season is limited to a maximum of 6-8 months, but long day length (16-20 hours) allows photosynthesis.

Annual precipitation 320 mm

SOIL

The main soil type is a podzol.
- Leaching by snowmelt.
- Raw acid humus p.H. 4.5-5.5.
- Very few earthworms, due to acidity, therefore little mixing of horizons.
- Thick litter layer due to low temperatures, and resistant acidic nature of needles.

Thin organic layer — Organic matter
— Silica
Ash-grey alleviated horizon — Ea
Dark brown depositer layer containing humus, clay, Fe, and Al — Bfe
Bedrock — C

VEGETATION

- Trees are evergreen - green throughout the year - therefore they are able to photosynthesise when temperatures rise above 3°C.
- The conical shape enables the trees to shed snow and reduce rocking by wind.
- Needle leaves reduce water loss.
- Forests usually contain only one main type of tree.
- Pine favours sandy soils, spruce damper soils.
- Ground vegetation is limited because it is too dark.

Low temperatures and slow rates of weathering produce large stores of nutrients in the litter layer

Population composition and population pyramids

POPULATION COMPOSITION

Population composition refers to any characteristic of the population. This includes the age, sex, ethnicity (race), language, occupational structure, and religious make up.

In the UK 19% of the population are aged under the age of 15 years and 16% are aged over the age of 65 years. This is different for ethnic groups. Among Whites 19% are in the under-15 group and 21% over-60 group. By contrast, among Pakistanis and Bangladeshis the proportions are 45% and 3%.

Population composition is important because it tells us about population growth. It helps planners to find out how many services and facilities, such as schools and hospitals, they will need to provide in the future.

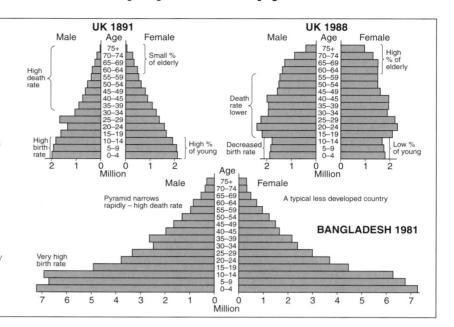

COMBINED POPULATION PYRAMIDS IN SOUTH AFRICA

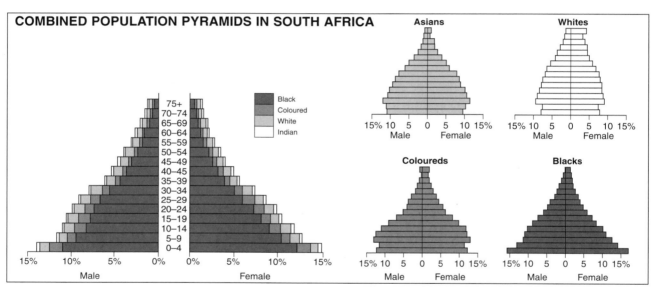

THE DEPENDENCY RATIO

The dependency ratio measures the working population and the dependent population. It is worked out by a formula:

$$\frac{\text{Population aged} \leq 15 + \text{population aged} \geq 60 \quad \text{(the dependents)}}{\text{Population aged 16-59} \quad \text{(the workers)}}$$

It is very crude. For example, many people stay on at school after the age of 15 and many people work after the age of 60. But it is a useful measure to compare countries.
- In the developed world there is a high proportion of elderly.
- In the developing world there is a high proportion of youth.

These can be shown on a triangular graph.

LDCs Less developed countries
MDCs More developed countries

UK   United Kingdom
Fr   France
Sw   Sweden
Jp   Japan
Bo   Bolivia

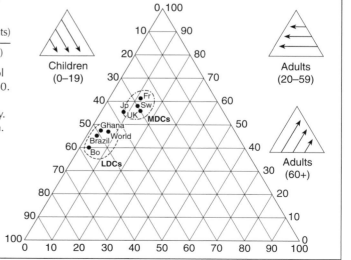

Population distribution and density

POPULATION DISTRIBUTION

Population distribution refers to where people live. On a global scale
- 75% of the population live within 1,000 km of the sea
- 85% live in areas less than 500m high
- 85% live between latitudes 68°N and 20°N
- less than 10% live in the southern hemisphere

The most favoured conditions include
- fertile valleys
- a regular supply of water
- a climate which is not too extreme
- good communications

Disadvantaged areas include deserts (too dry), mountains (too steep), high latitudes (too cold) and rainforests (too infertile).

There is no such thing as a 'best' climate - many people live in south east Asia, and this has a monsoonal climate, with hot, wet seasons and hot, dry seasons.

The higher the column on the map, the greater the population density.

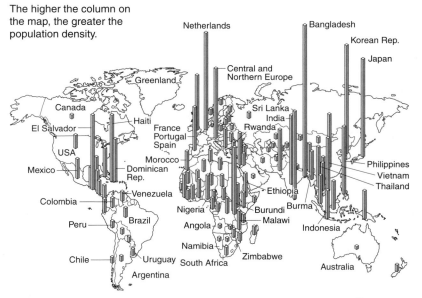

High-rises – relative population densities around the world (people per km²)

CASE STUDY: NATIONAL DISTRIBUTION IN THE UK, 1991

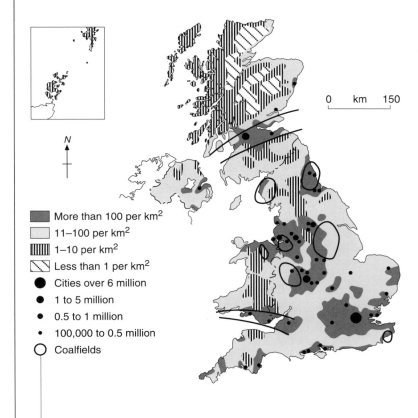

- More than 100 per km²
- 11–100 per km²
- 1–10 per km²
- Less than 1 per km²
- ● Cities over 6 million
- ● 1 to 5 million
- ● 0.5 to 1 million
- • 100,000 to 0.5 million
- ○ Coalfields

Explanation
- Coalfields were initially important to the rapid growth of industrial towns and subsequent agglomeration - they provided pools of skilled labour, large markets, industrial linkages, and inertia.

POPULATION DENSITY

Population density refers to the number of people per square km.

In the UK, population densities of over 100 per square km are found in parts of the South East, the Midlands, and the North West. In parts of London, the density reaches over 4,300 per square km. Many of the former coalfields have high population densities. By contrast, parts of Scotland have densities of less than 1 per square km. This is because it is a remote area with a harsh climate. There are very few opportunities in many parts of Highland Scotland.
- The North West is the most densely populated region with 868 people per square km.
- Scotland has 10% of the UK population on 35% of the UK land area.
- The South East has 33% of the UK's population on 10% of the UK's land.

CHANGING DISTRIBUTIONS

Counterurbanisation occurs when people move from larger towns and cities to smaller ones. This has led to a growth in small towns and rural areas.

Population growth

THE DEMOGRAPHIC TRANSITION MODEL (DTM)

The DTM describes how birth rates and death rates change over time. It is divided into four stages (and sometimes a fifth)

Stage 1 High stationary
- Birth rates and death rates are high and variable
- population growth fluctuates
- there are no countries now at this stage, although some indigenous (primitive) tribes still are
- the UK was at this stage until about 1750

Stage 2 Early expanding
- The birth rate remains high but the death rate comes down rapidly
- population growth is rapid
- countries such as Afghanistan, Sudan, and Libya are at this stage
- the UK passed through this stage by 1850

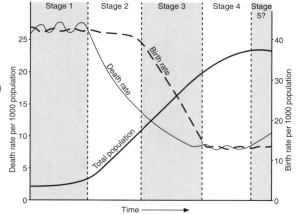

Stage 3 Late expanding
- The birth rate drops and the death rate remains low
- population growth continues but at a smaller rate
- Brazil and Argentina are at this stage
- the UK passed through this stage in about 1950

Stage 4 Low and variable
- Birth rates and death rates are low and variable
- population growth fluctuates
- the UK and most developed countries are now at this stage

Stage 5 Low and declining
- The birth rate is lower than the death rate
- the population declines

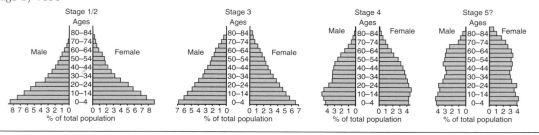

BIRTH RATES (the birth rate is the number of live births per thousand people per year)

Why do you get high birth rates?
Parents want children
- for labour
- to look after them in old age
- to continue the family name
- for prestige
- to replace other children who have died

Why do birth rates come down?
- children are very costly
- the government looks after people through pensions and health services
- more women want their own career
- there is more widespread use of family planning
- as the infant mortality rate comes down there is less need for replacement children

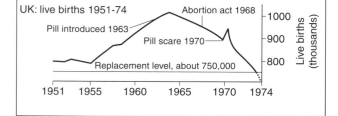

DEATH RATES (the death rate is the number of deaths per thousand people per year)

Why are death rates high?
- lack of clean water
- lack of food
- poor hygiene and sanitation
- overcrowding
- contagious (infectious) diseases
- poverty

Why do death rates decline?
- clean water
- reliable food supply
- good hygiene and sanitation
- lower population densities
- better vaccinations and health care
- rising standards of living

LIFE EXPECTANCY (YEARS)

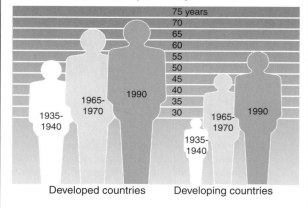

Population and resources

The world's population is growing very rapidly. 95% of population growth is taking place in less developed countries (LDCs). Population growth creates great pressures on governments to provide for their people; increased pressure on the environment; increased risk of famine and malnutrition; and greater differences between the richer countries and the poorer countries.

The rise of world population

In 1988, 36% of the population was under 15, 42% lived in urban areas

After beginning of 19th century: 1bn

Mid-17th century: 500,000

2022: 8bn
2010: 7bn
1999: 6bn
1987: 5bn
1974: 4bn
1960: 3bn
1918-1927: 2bn

Less developed countries

Developed countries

1650 1700 1750 1800 1850 1900 1950 2000 2050 2100

In 1798 Thomas Malthus predicted that population growth would be greater than the growth in food and resources. He said that food supply grew at a steady pace such as 1, 2, 3, 4, 5 and so on. By contrast, population grew at an increasing pace such as 1, 2, 4, 8, 16 and so on. If there was no attempt to reduce population growth, the result would be famine, war, and disease.

According to Malthus, population growth could be reduced by
• delayed age of marriage
• abstinence from sex.
(He was a vicar and was writing long before the widespread availability of contraceptives.)

A different view is that of Esther Boserup. She believed that people have the resources to increase food production. The greatest resources are knowledge and technology. When a need arises, someone will find a solution.

There have been many ways since Malthus's time that people have increased food production. These include
• draining marshlands
• reclaiming land from the sea
• cross breeding of cattle
• high yielding varieties of plants
• terracing on steep slopes
• growing crops in greenhouses
• using more sophisticated irrigation techniques
• making new foods such as soya
• making artificial fertilisers
• farming native species of crops and animals
• fish farming.

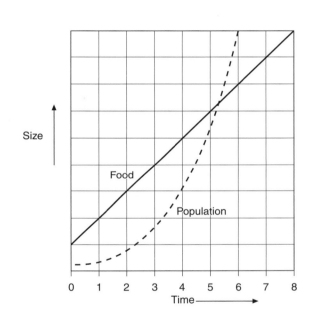

Size

Food

Population

0 1 2 3 4 5 6 7 8
Time ———→

VIEWS OF POPULATION GROWTH
There are two opposing views of the effects of this growth:

1 Neo-Malthusian

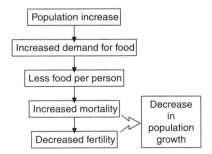

Expanding population means increasing food production causing environmental and financial problems.

2 Resource optimists (Boserup)

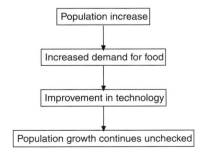

People are the ultimate resource - through innovation or intensification humans can respond to increased numbers.

Migration

Migration is a permanent change of residence with a complete change of community affiliations. Thus it does not include commuting (a daily movement to work), seasonal movements, or moving house in the same city.

Migrations are commonly divided into a number of types:
- forced or voluntary
- long distance or short distance
- international or internal.

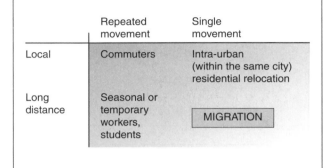

	Repeated movement	Single movement
Local	Commuters	Intra-urban (within the same city) residential relocation
Long distance	Seasonal or temporary workers, students	MIGRATION

PUSH AND PULL FACTORS

Migration is often explained by push factors and pull factors. **Push factors** are the negative features which cause a person to move away from a place. These include unemployment, low wages, and natural hazards. **Pull factors** are the attractions (whether real or just imagined) that exist at another place. Better wages, more jobs, and good schools are pull factors.

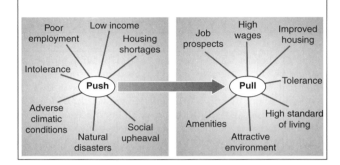

THE IMPACT OF MIGRATION

(a) Rural-urban migration in Zambia

Benefits	-to the destination	-for the migrants
	• young male labour	• higher wages
	• concentration of population	• amenities

Urban population pyramid

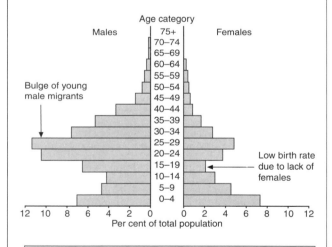

Per cent of total population

Costs	-to the destination	-for the migrants
	• pressure on services	• unemployment/ underemployment
	• pollution	• poor health
	• lack of money for development	• lack of housing
		• cycle of poverty

(b) Turkish immigrants in the Netherlands

Benefits	-to the destination	-for the migrants
	• cheap labour willing to do low-paid jobs	• chance of Western-style life
		• better education and health care

Population pyramid for Turkish migrants, 1981

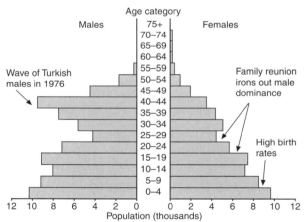

Population (thousands)

Costs	-to the destination	-for the migrants
	• demographic imbalance	• racism and hostility
	• provision of special educational services	• segregation in inner city
		• unemployment due to deindustrialisation

Major international migrations include
- Mexicans into the USA
- Turks into Germany
- Moroccans into France

Rural settlement

SITE
The site is the actual location on which settlements are built. Good sites include
- well drained, and free from flooding (dry point site)
- close to a reliable source of water (wet point site)
- defendable sites
- south facing slopes (warm sites)
- sheltered sites
- fertile land

SITUATION
The situation is the location of a settlement relative to other settlements and large physical features. For example, Oxford is situated in the Thames Valley between the Cotswolds and Chiltern Hills, about sixty miles north-west of London.

The situation of Corfe Castle
The site of Corfe Castle

- 🏘 farms (dispersed)
- 🏘 Corfe Castle (nucleated)
- ▒ high land
- ++++ railway
- —— road
- ⬯ river

THE SITE AND SITUATION OF CORFE CASTLE

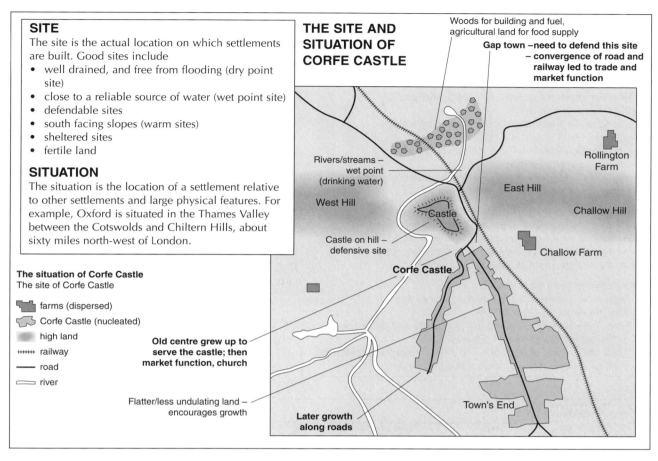

Woods for building and fuel, agricultural land for food supply

Gap town – need to defend this site – convergence of road and railway led to trade and market function

Rivers/streams – wet point (drinking water)

Rollington Farm

East Hill

West Hill

Challow Hill

Castle

Challow Farm

Castle on hill – defensive site

Corfe Castle

Old centre grew up to serve the castle; then market function, church

Flatter/less undulating land – encourages growth

Town's End

Later growth along roads

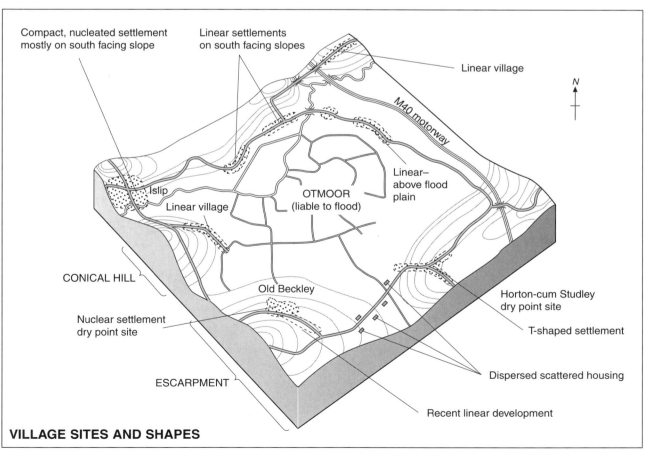

Compact, nucleated settlement mostly on south facing slope

Linear settlements on south facing slopes

Linear village

N

M40 motorway

Islip

Linear – above flood plain

Linear village

OTMOOR (liable to flood)

CONICAL HILL

Old Beckley

Horton-cum Studley dry point site

Nuclear settlement dry point site

T-shaped settlement

Dispersed scattered housing

ESCARPMENT

Recent linear development

VILLAGE SITES AND SHAPES

Rural settlements: function and change

CENTRAL PLACE THEORY

Central place theory is a model which describes the relative size and spacing of settlements.

Low order goods are low cost, everyday 'convenience' goods, such as newspapers or bread.

High order goods are expensive 'comparison' goods, such as cars and televisions.

The **range** is the maximum distance that people are prepared to travel to obtain a good or service.

The **threshold** population is the number of people needed to support a good or service.

The **sphere of influence** is the area that is served by a settlement.

Hamlets are the smallest settlements. They have low order goods which have a small range and threshold population.

Conurbations are the largest settlements. They contain many high order goods as well as low order goods. They have a high range and high threshold population.

Hierarchy has three main aspects:
1 High order settlements offer more functions and they are normally larger in size.
2 High order settlements occur less frequently and are spaced further apart than low order settlements.
3 There are a series of steps or levels in the hierarchy representing hamlets, villages, towns, cities, and conurbations.

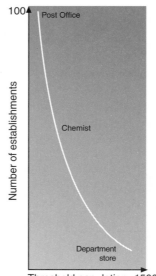

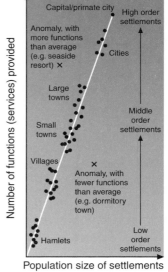

RURAL CHANGE

Many rural settlements are changing due to suburbanisation and counterurbanisation. Villages which are closest to large urban areas are changed the most.

Linear development
The tendency for large towns and cities to grow outwards along roads has been checked by the **green belt** policy.

Suburbanised villages
Dormitory or **commuter** villages with a residential workforce employed in urban areas.

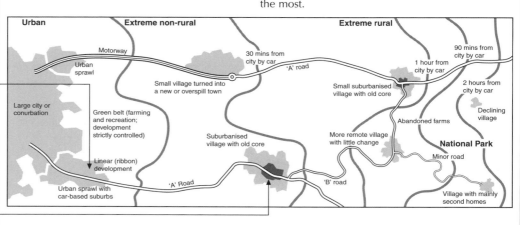

CASE STUDY: RURAL CHANGE IN THE GOWER PENINSULA

Accessible
• growth based on personal choice and planning decisions
• good links to Swansea and other villages

Large depopulation
Between 1971 and 1981 Rhossili lost 15% of its population and Llangennith 10%.

Inaccessible (extreme rural)
• depopulation
• some second or holiday homes

Repopulation
Reynoldston grew by 35% between 1971 and 1981. The village was chosen as an area for new housing.

Area of Outstanding Natural Beauty
• large rise in second or holiday homes

Extreme non-rural
• good links to Swansea resulted in considerable expansion
• villages grew in the sixties and seventies and have essentially lost their rural characteristics
• residents work in Swansea in non-rural jobs
• suburbanised residential structure

Rise in part-time residents
Oxwich had a 12% rise in holiday homes (accommodation let to different occupiers during the year). Port Eynon, which has the best road links, showed a 43% rise in second homes.

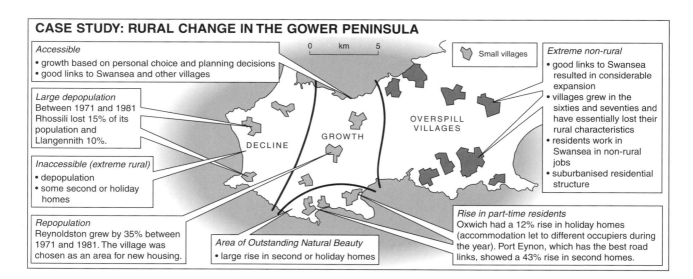

Urban land use

There are a number of models of urban structure. Every model is a simplification. We do not expect any city to 'fit' perfectly any of these models. But there are parts of all of these models which can be applied to most cities in the developed world.

Key for diagrams 1, 2 and 3
1 CBD (central business district)
2 Zone in transition/light manufacturing
3 Low-class residential
4 Medium-class residential
5 High-class residential
6 Heavy manufacturing
7 Outlying business district
8 Residential suburb
9 Industrial suburb
10 Commuter zone
Building age decreases outwards

1 CONCENTRIC ZONE MODEL (BURGESS, 1925)

- model based on Chicago in the 1920s
- the city is growing spatially due to immigration and natural increase
- the area around the CBD has the lowest status and highest density housing
- residents move outwards with increasing social class and their homes are taken by new migrants

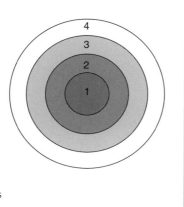

2 SECTOR MODEL (HOYT, 1939)

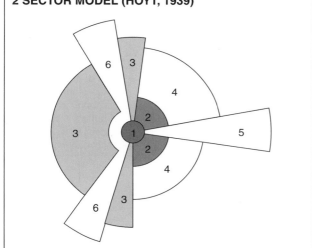

3 MULTIPLE-NUCLEI MODEL (HARRIS AND ULLMAN, 1945)

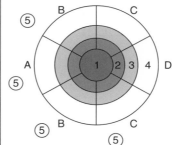

4 MANN'S SECTOR AND ZONE MODEL

- the east part of the city is the industrial end
- the west end is the richer side of a city
- prevailing westerly winds carry pollution and waste material eastwards
- there is increasing size of house and socioeconomic status with increasing distance from the city

1 CBD
2 Zone in transition
3 Zone of small terraced houses in sectors C and D, large old houses in sector A
4 Post-1918 residential areas with post-1945 development mainly on edge
5 Commuting distance villages

A Middle-class sector
B Lower-middle class sector
C Working-class sector (and main municipal housing areas)
D Industry and lowest working-class areas

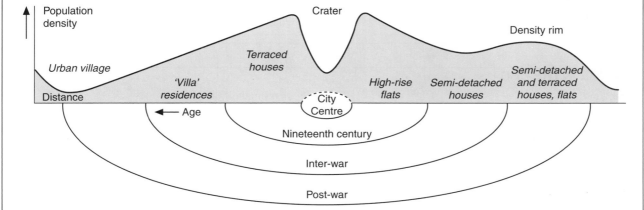

THE DENSITY CURVE WITH A HIGH-DENSITY RIM

There are low residential densities in the city centre. Peak residential densities are beyond the central area, in the inner city. The rise in densities in the outer suburbs is due to the development of council housing estates in the last thirty years.

The central business district (CBD)

The central business district (CBD) is generally at the heart of the city and is the focus for the urban transport system. It is the centre of the city's commercial, social, and cultural life. It possesses a number of clearly defined characteristics.

CHARACTERISTICS OF THE CBD

Vertical zoning
- land use changes within multi-storey blocks
- shops and services occupy ground floors

Absence of manufacturing
- a few specialised activities such as newspapers

Concentration of offices
- central location needed for clients and workforce
- offices tend to locate in zones

Multi-storey development
- high land values encourage buildings to grow upwards
- the real area of the CBD should therefore be measured in floor space rather than ground space

Low residential population
- high bid rents mean that few people live in the CBD
- there may be some luxury flats, especially in large cities

Pedestrianisation
- since the 1960s urban traffic management has limited the movement of vehicles within the CBD
- pedestrianisation has made shopping safer but some town centres have lost character

Concentration of retailing
- accessibility attracts shops with wide ranges and high threshold populations
- department stores and high threshold chains dominate in the centre
- specialist shops occupy less accessible sites

Comprehensive redevelopment
- the clearance of sites for complete rebuilding
- sometimes the CBD is extended into the inner city, causing conflict with residents
- redevelopment can also shift the centre of the CBD, causing some businesses to decline

CHANGE IN THE CBD

Attractions of the CBD

- maximum accessibility
- large threshold population
- prestige
- clustering of functions - legal, financial, entertainment
- range of goods and services available

Problems in the CBD

- lack of space
- high cost of land
- congestion
- lack of sites
- planning restrictions
- strict government control

These features can be related to most cities.

Inner cities

The inner city is the area surrounding the central business district. It is sometimes called the 'zone in transition' or the 'twilight zone'.

Problems in the inner city
- old, poor quality housing
- lack of recreational space
- crime
- graffitti
- air pollution
- decline of manufacturing industry
- ageing population
- racial conflict
- high rates of immigrants
- a lack of services
- road congestion
- unemployment

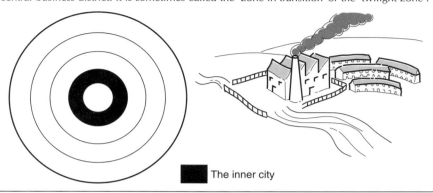

■ The inner city

URBAN REDEVELOPMENT

The main types of urban redevelopment include
- slum clearance - the removal of old, poor quality housing

- peripheral housing estates - new estates on the edges (peripheries) of towns
- regeneration and modernisation - upgrading of existing housing stock

CASE STUDY: URBAN REDEVELOPMENT IN GLASGOW

Slum clearance (1957-74)
- comprehensive redevelopment of the tenement areas (Govan, Gorbals, Royston) of the inner city, which were cleared by bulldozers

- existing communities were broken up and forced to relocate to bleak estates on the edge of Glasgow

Peripheral council housing (1952 to the early 1970s)
Problems - post-war housing was high density (700 persons per acre) and poorly maintained, with a lack of basic amenities (over 50% of all houses with no bath) and infested by vermin, especially rats

Policy - 500,000 people were dispersed to new towns like East Kilbride and Cumbernauld and peripheral council housing at Castlemilk and Drumchapel

Evaluation - estates lacked amenities; displaced and divided communities; poor design and rushed construction led to problems of damp and vermin

TOP-DOWN
Government-generated initiatives which attempt to change social or economic structure.

The GEAR project (1976-87)
Problems - Glasgow Eastern Area Renewal (GEAR) was a response to the mistakes of slum clearance and peripheral estates

Policy - modernisation rather than demolition with newly-built housing (2000 private homes) combining with existing housing

Evaluation - succeeded in attracting 300 new factories and improving housing (1200 homes were rehabilitated); stopped out-migration of residents; although 'job-rich', most jobs are taken by commuters

Transport
- Glasgow's ambitious transport policy included the construction of one of the UK's few 'urban freeways', the M8

- improved communications led to an increase in commuting and the loss of some good quality inner city housing

Deprivation
- despite planning policies, deprivation still exists, especially in the peripheral housing schemes

- many believe that long-term unemployment cannot be solved by urban planners

- others argue that newer policies like GEAR ignore social problems

Slum clearance high
• Deprivation (1991)
.... Planning Priority Area

Drumchapel
Maryhill
Possilpak
Royston
Easterhouse
M8 Govan
Haghill
Gorbals
GEAR
Pollok
Castlemilk

0   km   4

The Govan initiative (1987-94)
Problems - factory closure; decay and decline of housing stock; environmental damage by M8 motorway

Solutions - small-scale developments, new businesses, environmental improvements (landscaping), education and training for resident workforce

Success/failure - rebirth of local shipyard provided jobs for local workers; 'bottom-up' approach served the needs of the community

BOTTOM-UP
Locally-based initiatives including small-scale social action.

New towns and green belts

CASE STUDY: THE GREATER LONDON PLAN

Until the mid-1960s the basis for planning in the South-East was the 1944 Greater London Plan ('The Abercrombie Plan'). The plan was set up to solve a number of problems:

- London was too large. Too many of the UK's jobs were centred on London.
- Other areas were suffering unemployment. London was congested. Many dwellings were slums.

New Towns

New Towns Act, 1946

- New Towns were set up to provide alternatives to London in terms of housing and employment

- eight New Towns were created around London - with target populations of between 25,000 and 80,000

- 28 settlements were expanded to take another 535,000 migrating Londoners ('expanded towns')

Green belts

Green Belt Act, 1938

- a zone of land around London within which building is controlled

- set up to stop the sprawl of London and the merging of neighbouring towns, to protect farmland, and to restrict harmful activities on rural-urban fringe

- 25 km wide; has many towns within it, which can only expand by infilling the spaces between existing buildings

NEW TOWNS - SUCCESS OR FAILURE?

- First wave New Towns were close enough to London to allow daily commuting
  - they helped to relieve the housing problem
  - but added to congestion

- Second wave New Towns were much bigger and were built further out and have become independent growth poles, e.g. Milton Keynes.

GREEN BELTS - SUCCESS OR FAILURE?

- Green belts have succeeded in protecting many rural areas from urban sprawl.

- Green belts have caused many problems, such as:
  - increased commuting as urban dwellers relocate outside the green belt
  - house prices inside the Green belt rise
  - much of the green belt is poor quality and not worth preserving
  - market forces have seen planning regulations relaxed, e.g. the construction of the M25

HOW NEW TOWNS AND GREEN BELTS WORK

The city cannot grow so New Towns are built outside the Green Belt to house workers and their families

Many people commute from the New Town across the Green Belt to the city for work

Green Belts prevent urban sprawl (spread) and provide land for recreation and farming

Expanded towns are existing towns which are enlarged

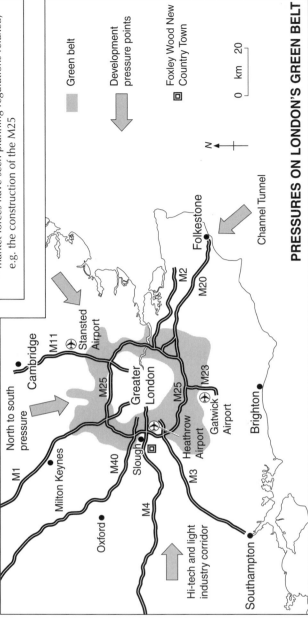

Green belt

Development pressure points

⊡ Foxley Wood New Country Town

0 km 20

N

PRESSURES ON LONDON'S GREEN BELT

Supercities

There are an increasing number of very large cities with populations of over 5 million people. These are known as 'supercities'. In most cases these are 'primate cities'. This means that they dominate a country in terms of size, location of manufacturing, investment, and power. Very often, supercities are ports with important trade functions or centres of former empires. However, being big is not always a good thing. The quality of life in many large cities is very poor. There are severe problems with

- housing
- employment
- water and sanitation
- health
- education

THE QUALITY OF LIFE IN SUPERCITIES

	Population (millions)	Murders per 100,000	% of income spent on food	Persons per room	% of houses with water/ electricity	Tele- phones per 100 people	% of children secondary school	Infant deaths per 1000 live births	Noise levels (1-10)	Traffic flow mph in rush hour	Quality of life score
Tokyo	28.7	1.4	18	0.9	100	44	97	5	4	28.0	81
Mexico City	19.4	27.8	41	1.9	94	6	62	36	6	8.0	38
New York	17.4	12.8	16	0.5	99	56	95	10	8	8.7	70
Sao Paulo	17.2	26.0	50	0.8	100	16	67	37	6	15.0	50
Osaka	16.8	1.7	18	0.6	98	42	97	5	4	22.4	81
Seoul	15.8	1.2	34	2.0	100	22	90	12	7	13.8	58
Moscow	13.2	7.0	33	1.3	100	39	100	20	6	31.5	64
Bombay	12.9	3.2	57	4.2	85	5	49	59	5	10.4	35
Calcutta	12.8	1.1	60	3.0	57	2	49	46	4	13.3	34
Buenos Aires	12.4	7.6	40	1.3	86	14	51	21	3	29.8	55

© Source: Population Crisis Committee

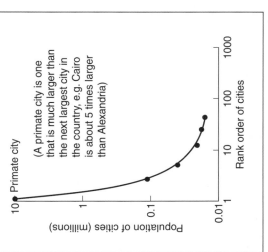

(A primate city is one that is much larger than the next largest city in the country, e.g. Cairo is about 5 times larger than Alexandria)

Urban problems and solutions: Cairo

POPULATION GROWTH IN CAIRO

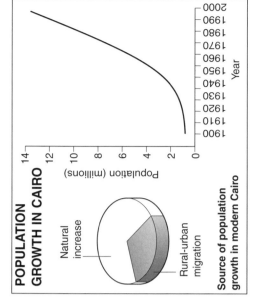

Natural increase

Rural-urban migration

Source of population growth in modern Cairo

SOLUTIONS

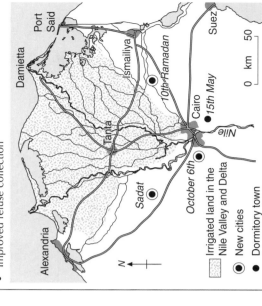

- New satellite (edge) and dormitory (without main services and functions) towns such as 10th Ramadan City and 15th May City
- Massive ring road to relieve pressure on the city centre
- Metro line with over one million commuters every day
- Repair sewers
- Improved refuse collection

N
0 km 50

Irrigated land in the Nile Valley and Delta
● New cities
• Dormitory town

Port Said

Damietta
Ismailiya
Suez
10th Ramadan
Tanta
Cairo
15th May
Nile
October 6th
Sadat
Alexandria

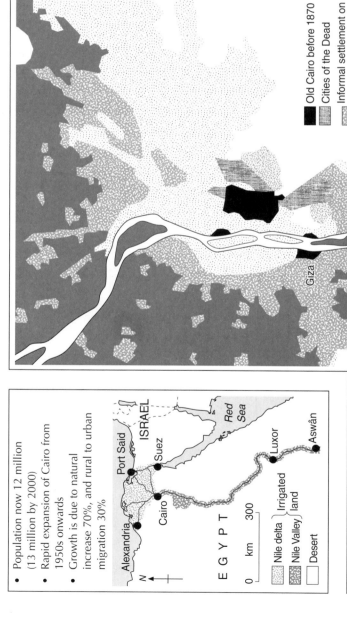

Giza

N
0 km 10

■ Old Cairo before 1870
▥ Cities of the Dead
▨ Informal settlement on green land
░ Squatter settlement on state-owned land
□ Other settlement
▒ Built-up area 1989

- Population now 12 million (13 million by 2000)
- Rapid expansion of Cairo from 1950s onwards
- Growth is due to natural increase 70%, and rural to urban migration 30%

N
0 km 300

E G Y P T

▦ Nile delta ⎱ Irrigated
▩ Nile Valley ⎰ land
□ Desert

Port Said
ISRAEL
Suez
Red Sea
Alexandria
Cairo
Luxor
Aswân

PROBLEMS

1 Housing
   - informal housing (self-built, shanty, temporary) accounts for 80% of Cairo's housing
   - 2-3 million people live in the Cities of the Dead (graveyards)
   - Population density reaches over 30,000 per square km
2 Traffic congestion
3 Lack of jobs / low salaries
4 Water and air pollution
5 Vehicle fumes - smog
6 Ground water pollution
7 Leaking sewers
8 Rotting buildings
9 Environmental hazards
   - in 1992 30,000 buildings collapsed in an earthquake

Farming systems

Farming systems

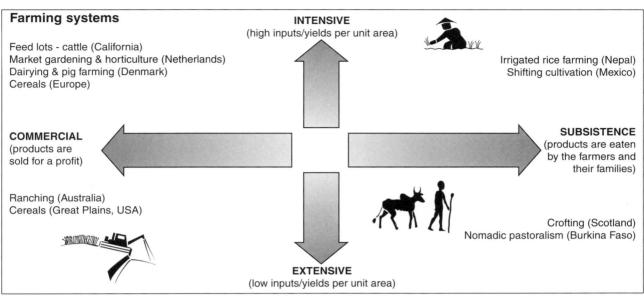

Feed lots - cattle (California)
Market gardening & horticulture (Netherlands)
Dairying & pig farming (Denmark)
Cereals (Europe)

INTENSIVE
(high inputs/yields per unit area)

Irrigated rice farming (Nepal)
Shifting cultivation (Mexico)

COMMERCIAL
(products are
sold for a profit)

SUBSISTENCE
(products are eaten
by the farmers and
their families)

Ranching (Australia)
Cereals (Great Plains, USA)

Crofting (Scotland)
Nomadic pastoralism (Burkina Faso)

EXTENSIVE
(low inputs/yields per unit area)

INTENSIVE SUBSISTENCE
Shifting cultivation: Poppalucan Indians, Mexico

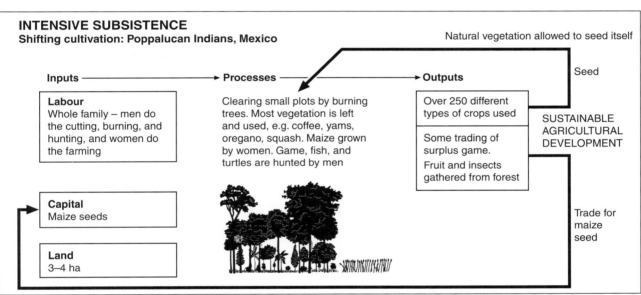

Natural vegetation allowed to seed itself

Inputs ⟶ **Processes** ⟶ **Outputs**

Labour
Whole family – men do
the cutting, burning, and
hunting, and women do
the farming

Clearing small plots by burning
trees. Most vegetation is left
and used, e.g. coffee, yams,
oregano, squash. Maize grown
by women. Game, fish, and
turtles are hunted by men

Over 250 different
types of crops used

Some trading of
surplus game.

Fruit and insects
gathered from forest

Seed

SUSTAINABLE
AGRICULTURAL
DEVELOPMENT

Trade for
maize
seed

Capital
Maize seeds

Land
3–4 ha

INTENSIVE COMMERCIAL
Pig farming in Denmark

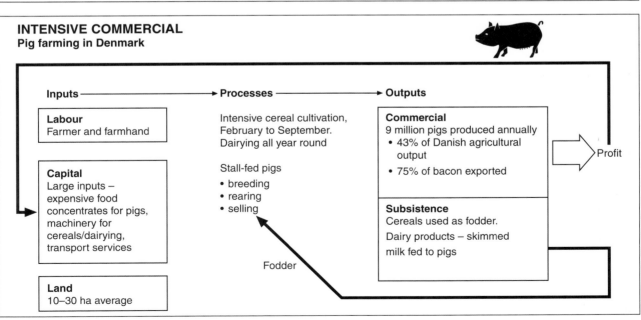

Inputs ⟶ **Processes** ⟶ **Outputs**

Labour
Farmer and farmhand

Intensive cereal cultivation,
February to September.
Dairying all year round

Stall-fed pigs
• breeding
• rearing
• selling

Commercial
9 million pigs produced annually
• 43% of Danish agricultural
output
• 75% of bacon exported

Profit

Capital
Large inputs –
expensive food
concentrates for pigs,
machinery for
cereals/dairying,
transport services

Subsistence
Cereals used as fodder.
Dairy products – skimmed
milk fed to pigs

Fodder

Land
10–30 ha average

Agriculture in the British Isles

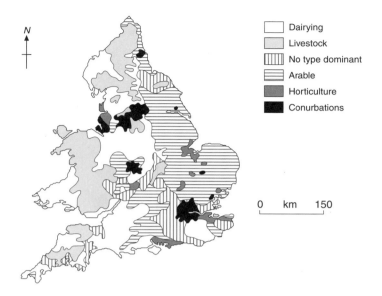

Legend:
- Dairying
- Livestock
- No type dominant
- Arable
- Horticulture
- Conurbations

0   km   150

Sheep farming in Wales

Physical factors
- Cool summers and cold winters prevent the growing of arable crops. The temperature promotes growth.
- High rainfall, ≥ 2000 mm, is too much for arable crops and produces grass instead.
- Soils are often thin, infertile and easily eroded.
- Hilly land prevents the use of much machinery.

Human factors
- There is some limited support for sheep farmers, but it is not as great as for arable farmers.
- The area is quite remote and isolated, and far from the main markets.
- Decreased demand for red meat products, such as lamb, due to health reasons.
- Small amounts of capital inputs.
- The area suffered from nuclear fallout after the nuclear disaster at Chernobyl in 1986.

Cereal farming in East Anglia

Physical factors
- Warm summers, > 20°C, favour the ripening of crops.
- Low rainfall, <600 mm, but it falls mostly in Spring and Summer when plants need it.
- Fertile boulder clay is good for arable farming.
- Flat land allows the use of machinery.

Human factors
- Government (CAP) support for cereals.
- Good communications (M11, Felixstowe port).
- Increased demand for cereal products.
- Lots of capital inputs (money, seeds, fertiliser, and pesticides).

Market gardening in the Vale of Evesham

Physical factors
- Much of the crops are under greenhouses so temperatures can be controlled. In other places, such as near Cheddar Gorge, south-west slopes are favoured because they are warmer.
- In greenhouses the water can be controlled. Some plants are grown in water - this is known as hydroponics.
- Soils are treated with lots of fertiliser.

Human factors
- Good communications (M5) and access to a large, wealthy urban market.
- Large demand for products such as strawberries, lettuces, tomatoes, raspberries, apples.
- Very high levels of capital inputs (money, seeds, fertiliser, and pesticides).

Common Agricultural Policy

The **Common Agricultural Policy** was developed to achieve four main goals:
1 To increase agricultural **productivity** and **self-sufficiency**.
2 To ensure a **fair standard of living** for farmers.
3 To **stabilise markets**.
4 To ensure food was available to consumers at a **fair price**.

The CAP achieved its main aim of increasing food supply by **guaranteed prices** and **intervention buying and storage**, i.e. a guaranteed market. This led to **intensification**, **specialisation**, and **concentration** of agricultural activities in the better suited areas.

CAP REFORM

The CAP created huge surpluses - by the early 1990s, 33 million tons of cereal, 2200 million litres of wine, and 8 million tonnes of beef had to be stored. The cost of storing butter alone was over £5 million per week.

In 1992, the CAP was reformed. Surplus production was **inefficient** and **costly** to store. Subsidies were very large, and intensive farming was harming the environment. Changes included
- less price support
- quotas (limits to what farmers would produce)
- less intensive types of agriculture, and
- set-aside.

However, by 1995-6, owing to the reforms of the CAP and a series of very hot summers, agricultural surpluses had been drastically reduced.

The new food crisis

The worst food crisis since 1974 has left the world with only 53 days supply of grain. The world is seriously short of food and up to 35,000 children die from hunger related diseases every day. Worldwide grain stocks are well below the FAO's minimum necessary to safeguard world food security. In 1987 there was over 100 days' worth of food supplies, but in 1995 there were just over 50, and by the end of 1996 it will be below 50 days'.

World food production has lagged behind food consumption since 1993. The drought of 1995 has led to the lowest harvest of food per head since the mid-1970s. The blistering summer of 1995, the hottest recorded in many parts of the northern hemisphere, destroyed millions of crops. The drought in Spain entered its fourth year and wheat yields slumped to less than half of their 1994 levels.

The European food mountain is fast being eroded. Its grain mountain has fallen from 33 million tons in 1993 to just 5.5 million tons in 1995. The only significant surplus is the wine lake, at 120 million litres.

Europe is not producing enough food, partly as a result of the 1992 CAP reforms which increased the amount of set-aside. Plans to reduce set-aside to 10% of land, rather than 15% in 1995, are an attempt to increase food production.

CEREALS — 33 million tons
WINE — 2200 million litres
BEEF — 8 million tons

one view of the common agricultural policy

Farming in less developed countries (LDCs)

The importance of agriculture

Agriculture remains the main source of **employment** for most people in LDCs. However, its importance has declined in recent decades due to the growth of manufacturing and to decreased food prices. Nevertheless, it remains a vital part of many economies due to employment, **export earnings and food supply**.

Over three-quarters of the world's population live in LDCs, and in the poorest of these over 70% of the population are employed in agriculture.

The **global pattern** of agriculture in LDCs can be divided into three main groups.
1 Tropical Africa, Iran, Iraq, and Cambodia - extensive farming, shifting cultivation, low yields, limited inputs, limited mechanisation, and a small proportion of irrigation.
2 Latin America - a small proportion of cultivated land, high proportion of grain, low but increasing crop yields, and limited use of high yielding varieties (HYVs) and fertilisers.
3 South and East Asia - intensive cultivation, especially of rice, high yields, and much use of HYVs.

Farming systems in more developed countries (MDCs) and LDCs are very different. Agriculture in MDCs has more in common with manufacturing industry than it has with farming in LDCs. For example, much of it is run by companies, and is **capital intensive** (costs lots of money), highly **mechanised, large-scale, market-orientated** (geared to consumer demand), and **government involvement** is crucial. By contrast, agriculture in LDCs is typically **small-scale, labour intensive**, and **subsistence** by nature.

Non-permanent cultivation

| | Subsistence shifting cultivation |
| | Subsistence rotational fallow cultivation |

Livestock farming

	Nomadic herding
	Commercial extensive animal husbandry
	Little economic activity

Permanent cultivation

	Intensive mainly subsistence cultivation (rice dominant)
	Intensive mainly subsistence cultivation (rice unimportant)
P	Commercial plantation
M	Commercial Mediterranean agriculture
L	Mixed crop and livestock (subsistence and commercial)
	Extensive commercial grain farming

In LDCs there has been a decrease in production per head in many countries. Reasons include
- deteriorating environmental conditions
- poor farming practises
- over-population
- under-population, as in Rwanda, where there were not enough people to harvest crops from the fields
- the neglect of the agricultural sector by the government.

In parts of Africa, declining farmyields are widespread. At the heart of the problem is the fact that population growth exceeds agricultural production. Potential solutions are mostly related to intensification such as double cropping (two crops a year), irrigation, increased use of fertilisers and greenhouses. But such developments are neither widespread nor even. For example, there is a very uneven pattern of fertiliser use with a large increase in Asia (especially China, India and Bangladesh) but not in Africa.

The green revolution

THE PROBLEM
Population growth is more rapid than the growth of food production. In India, for example, by 2000 AD the population will reach 1 billion people and food production will need to increase by 40% to match demand. But much of India's land is of limited potential.

THE SOLUTION?
The **green revolution** is the application of science and technology to increase crop productivity. It includes a variety of techniques such as genetic engineering to produce higher yielding varieties (HYVs) of crops and animals, mechanisation, pesticides, herbicides, chemical fertilisers, and irrigation water.

HYVs are the flagship of the green revolution. During 1967-8 India adopted Mexican Rice IR8 which yielded twice as much grain as traditional varieties. However, it required large amounts of water and fertiliser. Up to 55% of India's crops are now HYVs and 85% of the Philippines' crops are HYVs. By contrast only 13% of Thailand's crops are HYVs.

THE SPREAD OF HYVs

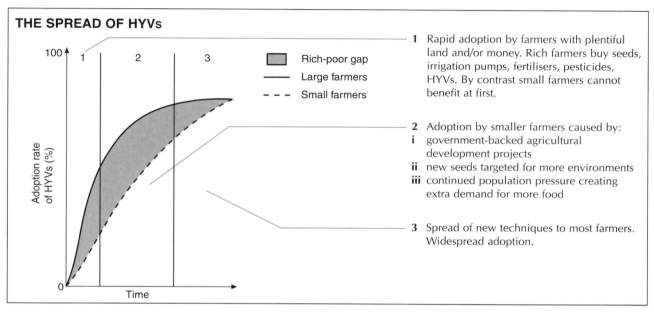

1 Rapid adoption by farmers with plentiful land and/or money. Rich farmers buy seeds, irrigation pumps, fertilisers, pesticides, HYVs. By contrast small farmers cannot benefit at first.

2 Adoption by smaller farmers caused by:
i government-backed agricultural development projects
ii new seeds targeted for more environments
iii continued population pressure creating extra demand for more food

3 Spread of new techniques to most farmers. Widespread adoption.

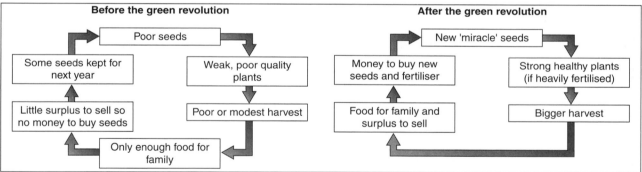

THE CONSEQUENCES
The main benefit is that more food can be produced:
• yields are higher
• up to three crops can be grown each year
• more food should lead to less hunger
• more exports create more foreign currency

However, there are many problems:
• not all farmers adopt HYVs - some cannot afford the cost
• as the cost rises, indebtedness increases
• rural unemployment has increased due to mechanisation
• irrigation has led to salinisation - 20% of Pakistan's and 25% of Central Asia's irrigated land is affected by salt
• soil fertility is declining as HYVs use up all the nutrients; these can be replenished by fertilisers, but this is expensive
• LDCs are dependent on many developed countries for the inputs

Changes in South India: the effects of the green revolution	
Use of fertiliser	+138%
Human labour	+111%
Paddy rice	+91%
Sugar cane	+41%
Income	+20%
Subsistence food	-90%
Energy efficiency	-25%
Casual employment	-66%

Agriculture and environmental issues

SOIL EROSION

- Over one-third of arable land in the UK is at risk of soil erosion
- Sandy and sandy-loam soils with a slope angle of more than 3° are particularly vulnerable
- Soil losses are up to 250 t/ha in the South Downs, 160 t/ha in Norfolk and 150 t/ha in West Sussex

The potential for soil erosion has increased considerably in recent years for a number of reasons:

1 Spread of arable land use into pastoral areas
2 Hedgerow removal
3 Ploughing and draining of peaty soils
4 Afforestation leaves bare ground between young trees
5 Increased recreational pressure in rural areas

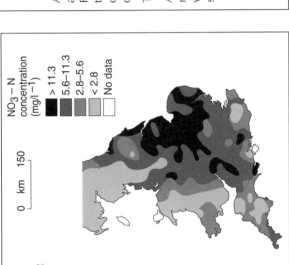

Potential for erosion by rainfall

Low
- < 700
- 700–900
- 900–1100
- 1100–1300
- > 1300
High

0   km   150

Nitrate pollution

Increased levels of nitrates in ponds and streams can cause eutrophication, i.e. nutrient enrichment.

Up to 5 million people in England and Wales are supplied with water with high rates of nitrates. This is linked with

- high rates of stomach cancer
- blue baby syndrome, due to oxygen starvation in the bloodstream

Solutions include

1 A change in land use to pastoral farming
2 Less intensive arable agriculture
3 Less use of fertiliser
4 The use of cover crops in winter to absorb fertiliser

NO₃ – N concentration (mg/l⁻¹)

- > 11.3
- 5.6–11.3
- 2.8–5.6
- < 2.8
- No data

0   km   150

BSE

BSE (a disease in cows) and CJD (a disease in humans) belong to a rare group of diseases called spongiform encephalopathies. Most cases of CJD have occurred in places where BSE is more common. In 1996 10 cases of CJD were diagnosed.

The first case of BSE in Britain was in 1986. Most of the infection in cattle took place in the late 1980s and it peaked in 1992. BSE came into cattle when they ate meat that was infected with scrapie, a disease common in sheep. Cows that were fed on infected sheep tissue developed BSE. As these cows were then slaughtered, crushed, and fed back to other cows, some of these became infected.

Why did it affect the UK?

- Cattle carcasses in the UK are burnt at a relatively low temperature.
- Cattle in the UK derive up to 5% of their food from meat and bone meal.
- The government only offered a 50% grant for farmers to destroy infected animals. It is believed that this encouraged farmers to pass off sick animals as healthy and lengthened the period that humans were fed potentially infected beef.

As soon as other EU countries suspected that British animals might be spreading BSE they banned it. France and Ireland destroyed all animals in any herd that contained even one case of BSE. This did not occur in the UK. Up to 85% of beef herds and 40% of dairy herds remain unaffected by BSE.

To eradicate BSE could cost up to £15 billion.

About 850,000 cows are killed every year. These are mostly cattle that have come to the end of their working lives and are used for products such as sausages, pate, pies, and glue.

Number of BSE cases

- Britain: 161,663
- Switzerland: 206
- Ireland: 123
- Portugal: 31
- France: 13
- Germany: 4
- Italy: 2
- Oman: 2
- Canada: 1
- Denmark: 1
- Falkland Islands: 1

Industrial location

CLASSIFICATION

Primary industries The extraction of raw materials, e.g. mining, quarrying, farming, fishing, and forestry.

Secondary industries Manufacturing industries which involve the transformation of raw materials (or components) into finished products or semi-finished products, e.g. steelworks, the car industry, and high technology.

Tertiary industries These are concerned with providing a service to customers, e.g. transport, retailing, and medical and professional services.

Quaternary industries These provide information and expertise, e.g. universities, research and development, media, and political policy units.

CHANGING INDUSTRIAL STRUCTURE OVER TIME

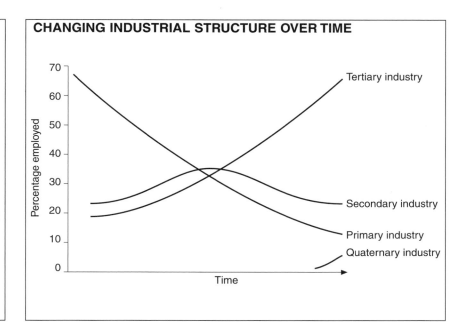

FACTORS INFLUENCING LOCATION

- Physical factors influenced industrial location in the nineteenth century.

- Old industrial regions were located where cheap energy and raw materials were found.

- Physical factors influenced mature industries like textiles, shipbuilding, and iron and steel.

- Transport costs and markets also influenced mature industries.

- In the 1990s, government policy and labour requirements have strong influences on industry.

- Industrial location is no longer country-specific and choices of location are global and strategic.

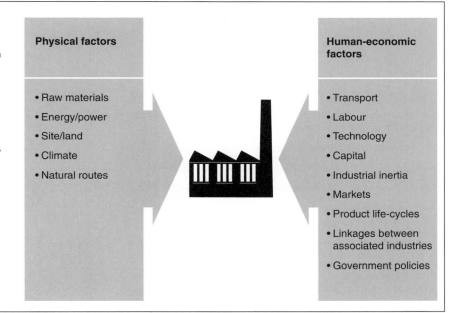

Agglomeration economies Savings which arise from the concentration of industries either together or close to linked activities.

Industrial inertia The survival of an industry in an area even though the initial advantages are no longer relevant.

Break-of-bulk location A location which takes its advantage from a position where there is forced transfer of freight from one transport medium to another, e.g. a port or rail terminal.

Greenfield site An industrial site located on the edge of an urban area in a place with no prior industrial use.

DEFINITIONS OF KEY WORDS

Rationalisation A reduction in the production capacity of a multi-plant firm by factory closure.

Transplant or branch plant An assembly plant owned and operated by a foreign-based company.

Transnational or multi-national corporation (TNC or MNC) A large, multi-plant firm with a worldwide manufacturing capability.

Research and development (R&D) The branch of a manufacturing firm concerned with the design and development of new products; R&D employs highly skilled workers.

The car industry

The world car industry can be viewed at three levels: the global, the national, and the regional. Each level is related but has different locational characteristics.

1 GLOBAL LOCATION

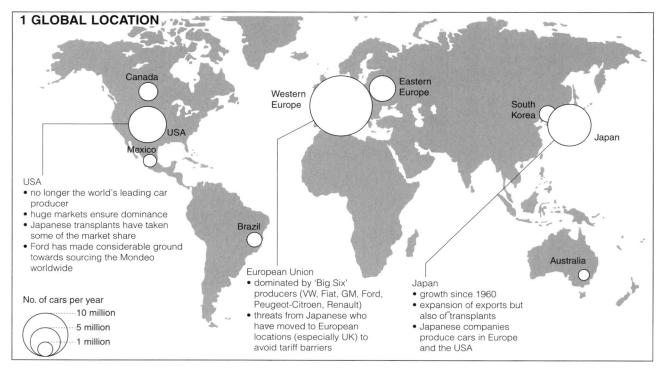

USA
- no longer the world's leading car producer
- huge markets ensure dominance
- Japanese transplants have taken some of the market share
- Ford has made considerable ground towards sourcing the Mondeo worldwide

No. of cars per year
- 10 million
- 5 million
- 1 million

European Union
- dominated by 'Big Six' producers (VW, Fiat, GM, Ford, Peugeot-Citroen, Renault)
- threats from Japanese who have moved to European locations (especially UK) to avoid tariff barriers

Japan
- growth since 1960
- expansion of exports but also of transplants
- Japanese companies produce cars in Europe and the USA

2 NATIONAL LOCATION - THE JAPANESE IN THE UK

The Japanese have shifted much of their production to Europe, especially the UK. There are two reasons for the move to Europe:

- to **avoid tariff barriers** and the restrictions of the Single Market

- to produce a car specifically for the **European market**

They have chosen the UK as their favoured location because of:

- the UK's **'open door' policy** - the government and most local authorities welcome Japanese investment

- **access to EU markets** - if the Japanese produce cars using 60% of their components sourced from Europe they avoid tariffs

- **regional assistance** - support available in intermediate and development areas can be a strong incentive

- **language and culture** - English is the universal business language

- **labour costs** - the UK has amongst the cheapest labour costs in Europe

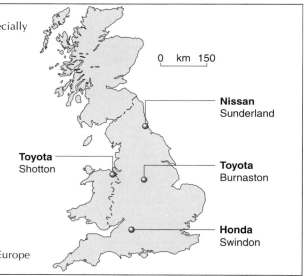

Nissan Sunderland

Toyota Shotton

Toyota Burnaston

Honda Swindon

3 REGIONAL LOCATION - TOYOTA

- In 1989 Toyota invested £700 million in a car plant in Burnaston, Derbyshire.

- Toyota has 160 European-based suppliers at present, from ten countries in the EU.

- The plant operates **just-in-time production** (orders and receives parts as they are needed) and purchases parts and components worth £113 million from within 50 miles of the plant.

Greenfield location
The plant is built on a disused airfield just outside Derby

Proximity of the components firms of the East Midlands
The East and West Midlands have a long tradition of supplying components to car firms

REASONS FOR LOCATION

Skilled workforce
By the end of 1992 the plant had received more than 20,000 job applications, 50% from within a 15 mile radius

Transport links to the EU
The plant lies alongside the M1/M6 link to the rest of England and the EU

The iron and steel industry

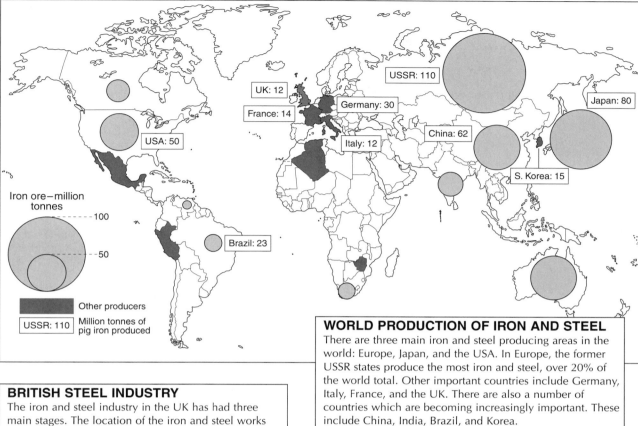

Iron ore—million tonnes

—100

—50

■ Other producers

USSR: 110 — Million tonnes of pig iron produced

World production figures:
- UK: 12
- France: 14
- Germany: 30
- USSR: 110
- Italy: 12
- China: 62
- Japan: 80
- S. Korea: 15
- USA: 50
- Brazil: 23

WORLD PRODUCTION OF IRON AND STEEL

There are three main iron and steel producing areas in the world: Europe, Japan, and the USA. In Europe, the former USSR states produce the most iron and steel, over 20% of the world total. Other important countries include Germany, Italy, France, and the UK. There are also a number of countries which are becoming increasingly important. These include China, India, Brazil, and Korea.

BRITISH STEEL INDUSTRY

The iron and steel industry in the UK has had three main stages. The location of the iron and steel works has changed with each of these stages.

1 Small-scale dispersed production - located close to raw materials, such as iron ore and charcoal, e.g. the Forest of Dean in Gloucestershire.

2 Coalfield locations - it took eight times more coal than iron ore to produce one tonne of steel. Therefore, the iron and steel industry moved to the coalfields to reduce transport costs, e.g. the South Wales coalfields.

3 Coastal locations - once the coal and iron ore reserves have gone, resources need to be imported. Coastal locations are better for the import of resources and the export of finished products, e.g. Teesside and Port Talbot.

- Many of the raw materials are imported from Poland, South Africa, the CIS, and Brazil.
- Steel plants have rationalised. They have become bigger and more competitive. However, smaller factories have closed down.
- Steel plants are now more mechanised - this creates unemployment.
- Plants are integrated - this means that different processes such as smelting and conversion to steel take place on the same plant.
- The demand for steel is decreasing. This is because there are other new materials such, as aluminium and plastics.
- There is increased competition between steel producers.
- There is a shift to Pacific Rim producers, that is countries in the East of Asia.

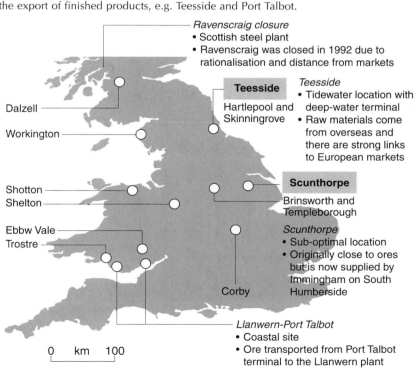

Ravenscraig closure
- Scottish steel plant
- Ravenscraig was closed in 1992 due to rationalisation and distance from markets

Teesside
Hartlepool and Skinningrove

Teesside
- Tidewater location with deep-water terminal
- Raw materials come from overseas and there are strong links to European markets

Scunthorpe
Brinsworth and Templeborough

Scunthorpe
- Sub-optimal location
- Originally close to ores but is now supplied by Immingham on South Humberside

Llanwern-Port Talbot
- Coastal site
- Ore transported from Port Talbot terminal to the Llanwern plant

Dalzell
Workington
Shotton
Shelton
Ebbw Vale
Trostre
Corby

0   km   100

High technology industries

DEFINITIONS AND CHARACTERISTICS

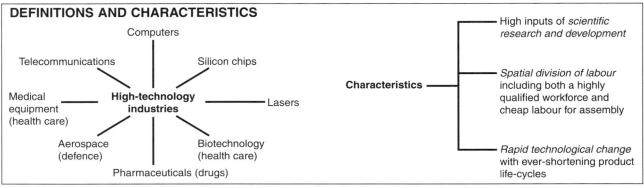

Computers

Telecommunications

Silicon chips

Medical equipment (health care) — **High-technology industries** — Lasers

Aerospace (defence)

Biotechnology (health care)

Pharmaceuticals (drugs)

Characteristics
- High inputs of *scientific research and development*
- *Spatial division of labour* including both a highly qualified workforce and cheap labour for assembly
- *Rapid technological change* with ever-shortening product life-cycles

HIGH TECHNOLOGY INDUSTRIES IN THE BRITISH ISLES

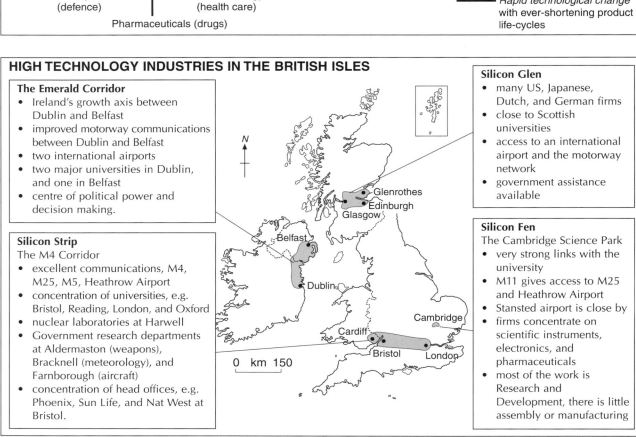

The Emerald Corridor
- Ireland's growth axis between Dublin and Belfast
- improved motorway communications between Dublin and Belfast
- two international airports
- two major universities in Dublin, and one in Belfast
- centre of political power and decision making.

Silicon Strip
The M4 Corridor
- excellent communications, M4, M25, M5, Heathrow Airport
- concentration of universities, e.g. Bristol, Reading, London, and Oxford
- nuclear laboratories at Harwell
- Government research departments at Aldermaston (weapons), Bracknell (meteorology), and Farnborough (aircraft)
- concentration of head offices, e.g. Phoenix, Sun Life, and Nat West at Bristol.

Silicon Glen
- many US, Japanese, Dutch, and German firms
- close to Scottish universities
- access to an international airport and the motorway network
- government assistance available

Silicon Fen
The Cambridge Science Park
- very strong links with the university
- M11 gives access to M25 and Heathrow Airport
- Stansted airport is close by
- firms concentrate on scientific instruments, electronics, and pharmaceuticals
- most of the work is Research and Development, there is little assembly or manufacturing

Map labels: Glenrothes, Edinburgh, Glasgow, Belfast, Dublin, Cardiff, Cambridge, Bristol, London

0   km 150

THE CAMBRIDGE PHENOMENON

Why Cambridge?
- prestige name and location
- attractive, landscaped sites
- links with the university
- highly qualified workforce
- links with related companies

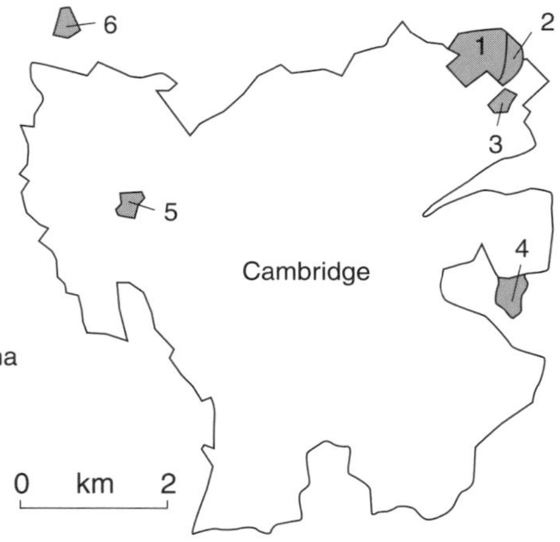

1 Cambridge Science Park
2 St Johns Innovation Park
3 Cambridge Buisness Arena
4 Quorum Buisness Park
5 Castle park
6 Histon Vision Park

Cambridge

0   km   2

Some side-effects
There have been many effects of Cambridge's success as a centre for high technology Research and Development.

The population has increased to over 100, 000. Land is being developed for housing and land prices are rising rapidly.

The number of students has risen and this increases the demand for housing. House prices have risen dramatically.

There are over 4,000 people on the council housing list, and less than 20% of young couples can afford a house in Cambridge.

New industry brings traffic and congestion. Cars move at an average speed of 14 mph during rush hour.

Many farmers are selling their land to property developers.

Services

SERVICES

The service sector includes all economic activities other than the production of goods. It includes insurance, banking, shipping, tourism, health care, refuse collection, entertainment, education, and retailing. Some services are provided by the State (e.g. NHS health care in the UK), while others are provided by the private sector (e.g. market research and advertising). Some jobs are extremely well paid (e.g. banking), others are very poorly paid (e.g. refuse collection). Many jobs are traditionally female (e.g. catering, cleaning), others male (e.g. transport).

TYPES OF SERVICES

A number of distinctions can be made:

1 Producer services are 'high order' activities, such as market research, management consultancy, financial, advertising, and legal functions, that are provided in a small number of highly developed metropolitan centres, generally capital cities, for other firms or organisations.

Consumer services are provided generally for people, e.g. health care, retailing, education, distribution, and refuse collection. These are more local in scale or 'low order'.

2 Non-basic services are provided for users in the local area.

Basic services are those which are provided for a market beyond the local economy, e.g. a national or a global market.

3 Private or **market** services are organised by independent companies, ranging from contract-cleaners and retailing, to banking and insurance. **State** or **non-market** services are organised by the government, such as central and local government, state health care, and education.

An area which depends upon **consumer non-basic services**, such as a post office or a supermarket, will attract little extra growth, whereas a **producer basic service**, such as an international bank, will make large exports. This will contribute to the region's and the nation's economic growth.

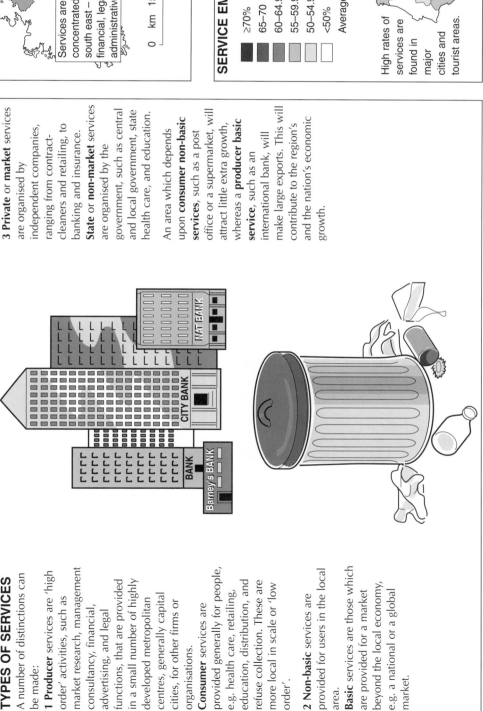

SERVICE EMPLOYMENT IN THE UK

%
- >75
- 70–74.99
- 65–69.99
- ≤64.99

Avg 72.9

Services are concentrated in the south east – the financial, legal and administrative centre

N

0   km   150

SERVICE EMPLOYMENT IN EUROPE

- ≥70%
- 65–70
- 60–64.9
- 55–59.9
- 50–54.9
- <50%

Average 63%

High rates of services are found in major cities and tourist areas.

N

0   km   1000

Newly industrialising countries

NEWLY INDUSTRIALISING COUNTRIES (NICS)

An NIC is characterised by:
- an increasing share of the world manufacturing output
- a significant growth in (manufactured) export production
- significant average annual growth in manufacturing production, between 4.5% in Portugal and 15% in South Korea.

Three main groups of NIC have been identified:
1. Asian 'tigers', such as Hong Kong, Singapore, South Korea, and Taiwan.
2. Latin American NICs, such as Brazil and Mexico.
3. European NICs, including Spain, Portugal, Greece, and the former Yugoslavia.

Some of these have been redefined e.g. Spain was classified as a developed country in 1983.

THE ROLE OF MULTINATIONAL COMPANIES (MNCS) IN NIC DEVELOPMENT

- MNCs facilitate economic development through their economic and political power, access to capital, skills and knowledge.
- MNCs heavily influence the type, scale, and location of manufacturing.

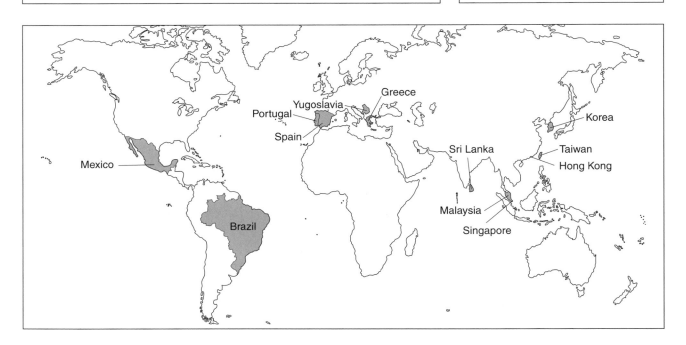

STAGES IN THE EMERGENCE OF AN NIC

1. **Traditional society**
   Labour intensive industries, low levels of technology. Local raw materials - food processing and textiles common.
2. **Import substitution industries (ISIs)**
   Reduction of expensive imports by development of home industries. Protectionist policies e.g. high trade tariffs on manufactured goods and car industry.
3. **Export orientated industries (EOIs)**
   High technology, capital intensive industries. R & D functions. Rapid growth and development.

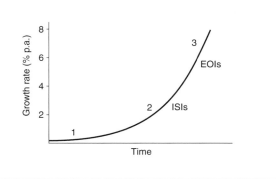

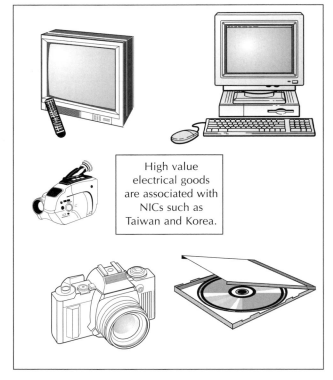

High value electrical goods are associated with NICs such as Taiwan and Korea.

The effects of rapid industrialisation

Economic effects

- Raises standard of living.
- Benefits the government and MNCs rather than the people.
- Change in labour force:
  (i) shift to manufacturing (secondary) industries, especially of young working population
  (ii) decline in agricultural employment and productivity; growth of rural unemployment
  (iii) increase in service industries, e.g. transport, retailing, and administration.
- Increased competition for land, raising land prices.

Child labour

- About 250 million children aged 5 years and over are working in LDCs (less developed countries). Nearly half of these work full-time.
- Up to 153 million children in Asia work.
- 40% of children in Africa work.
- India employs 100 million children, the largest in any country.
- Many children are employed in diamond polishing, match and fireworks making, slate, glass and textiles industries

In 1996 a ban on the use of child labour was imposed upon Bangladesh's garment industry. The ban was the result of intense US pressure. The US imports 60% of Bangladesh's garment exports. In addition, Bangladesh supplies 50% of the t-shirts in Europe. The use of child labour has been crucial in the spectacular growth of Bangladesh's textile industry. Nevertheless, in textiles factories in the USA, violation of immigrant workers' rights is widespread.

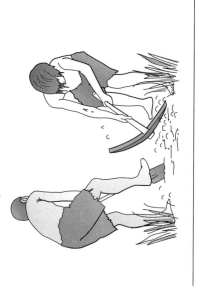

Social effects

Rural areas

- Social imbalance between affluent industrial minority/commercial workers and the rest of the population.
- Population changes, e.g. age-selective migration to urban areas.
- Decline of traditional values and lifestyles.
- Increased dependence on remittances from urban workers.
- Poor welfare systems.

Urban areas

- In-migration leads to rapid development of shanty towns, increased birth rates, and population growth.
- Concentration of unemployed and poor in shanty towns.
- High rates of crime, illiteracy, and disease in areas of poor housing
- Low levels of services.
- Unsatisfactory working conditions (sweatshops).

Environmental effects

- Resource exploitation can damage the natural environment and could lead to the destruction of whole habitats.
- Rivers polluted by industrial waste.
- Air pollution, e.g. in Taipei, Taiwan.
- Unsafe working practises may create environmental disasters, e.g. Bhopal in India in 1985, where toxic gas from the Union Carbide factory lead to widespread blindness in the area.
- Urban blight, e.g. derelict buildings, contaminated land.
- Limited environmental legislation.

Contrasts in development

WHAT IS DEVELOPMENT?

Development is difficult to define. It suggests
- economic growth
- stable population growth
- high standards of living
- high levels of technology
- employment
- good health
- adequate nutrition
- literacy
- high levels of GNP per head

More developed countries (MDCs), such as the UK, the USA and Japan, have high levels of these. By contrast, countries that are less developed (LDCs) have worse levels.

About 75% of the world's population live in LDCs and 25% in MDCs.

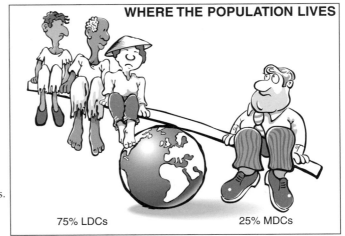

WHERE THE POPULATION LIVES

75% LDCs   25% MDCs

CLASSIFYING COUNTRIES

- The First World - Western Europe, North America, Australia, New Zealand, and Japan
- The Second World - State-controlled Communist countries, such as the former USSR
- The Third World - all the other less developed countries

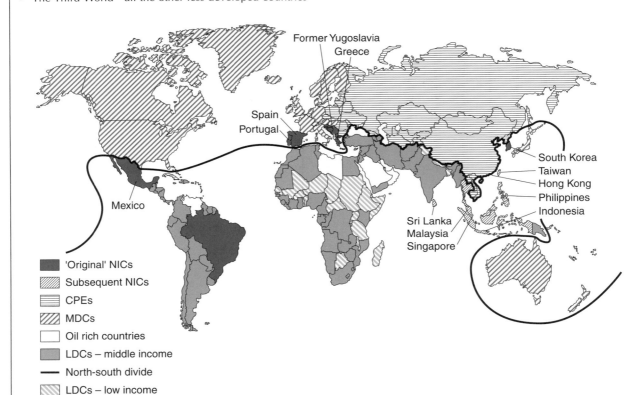

Former Yugoslavia
Greece
Spain
Portugal
Mexico
South Korea
Taiwan
Hong Kong
Philippines
Indonesia
Sri Lanka
Malaysia
Singapore

- 'Original' NICs
- Subsequent NICs
- CPEs
- MDCs
- Oil rich countries
- LDCs – middle income
- North-south divide
- LDCs – low income

A more popular and detailed way is as follows:
More Developed Countries (MDCs), such as the UK and the USA. These are the most 'developed' countries and have a high standard of living.
Less Developed Countries (LDCs), e.g. Namibia and India. These countries are at a lower stage of development and have a lower quality of life. These can be subdivided into middle income and low income LDCs.

Centrally Planned Economies (CPEs), socialist countries, such as North Korea, strictly controlled by the government. Living standards are higher than LDCs although freedom of speech is limited.
Oil rich countries, e.g. Saudi Arabia and Libya. These countries are very rich in terms of GNP per head, although it may not be distributed very evenly. Without oil many of these countries would be LDCs.
Newly Industrialising Countries (NICs), e.g. South Korea and Taiwan. Countries which have experienced rapid industrial, social, and economic growth since 1960. (By contrast old industrial countries (OICs) are usually MDCs).

Measuring development

One of the most common ways of measuring development is by the use of gross national product (GNP) per head. This is the total amount of a country's wealth divided by the number of people in it. GNP measures how wealthy a country is. The world map of GNP per head clearly shows that

- the MDCs of Western Europe, Japan, North America, and Australia have a much higher value than the LDCs such as India, Bangladesh, Nigeria, and Zimbabwe
- only 15% of the world's population live in areas with a high GNP per head, whereas 56% of the world's population live in areas with a low GNP per head.

However, average GNP per head has its shortcomings

- it hides regional variations
- it fails to take into account local costs of living
- it does not measure the social and environmental cost of development.

The World Bank prefers the use of Purchasing Power Parity (PPP), which is the level of GNP adjusted to local costs of living. This has the effect of lifting the position of most LDCs where the costs of living are lower and lowering the wealth of MDCs where the costs of living are higher.

Since 1990 the UN has used the Human Development Index (HDI) as a measure of development. This, they believe, is a more reliable and accurate measure of development as it includes three indices of well-being:

- life expectancy
- literacy and schooling
- PPP.

According to the latest figures, Canada has the highest HDI, with a value of 0.932 (1.0 is the maximum value), closely followed by Switzerland. MDCs dominate the higher levels of the HDI while LDCs, such as Afghanistan, Burkina Faso and Guinea, are at the bottom. As with GNP per head, national HDIs can conceal widespread inequalities.

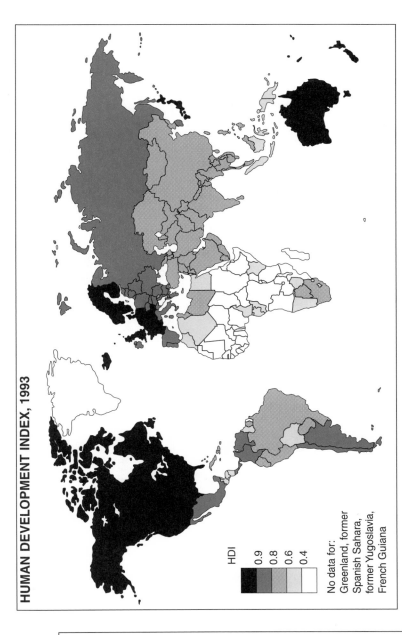

HUMAN DEVELOPMENT INDEX, 1993

HDI
- 0.9
- 0.8
- 0.6
- 0.4

No data for:
Greenland, former
Spanish Sahara,
former Yugoslavia,
French Guiana

HUMAN DEVELOPMENT INDEX, 1993

- 1.00 — Industrial countries
- **High HDI countries**
- 0.90 — East Asia excl. China
- Latin America, Caribbean
- 0.80 — Eastern Europe and CIS
- South East Asia and Pacific
- 0.70 — **Medium HDI countries**
- 0.60 — Arab states
- Developing countries
- 0.50 — South Asia
- **Low HDI countries**
- 0.40 — Sub-Saharan Africa
- 0.30 — Least developed countries

A COMPARISON OF THE HDI IN THE UK AND INDIA

	UK	India
Human Development Index	75.8	59.7
Adult literacy (%)	99	49.8
GDP per head ($)	16340	1150
Life expectancy (years)	75.6	59.7
Daily calorie supply (% of needs)	105	
Malnourished children ('000)	–	69 345
Malnourished children (%)	–	63
Infant mortality rate (per '000)	8	93
Cars per 100 people	41	0.7
% employment in agriculture	2	62
% employment in manufacturing	28	11
% employment in services	70	27
Income inequality: % of total		
Income that the poorest 40% have	17.3	21.3

Regional inequalities

There are large variations in the standards of living between different countries. There are also significant differences between regions of a country or a group of countries. The rich areas are often called the **core**, whereas the poorer areas are called the **periphery**.

In the European Union the core stretches from the South East region in the UK, through Belgium and Germany, to northern Italy. This area has been called the **hot banana**. The poorer regions include Greece, Spain, Portugal, and Ireland.

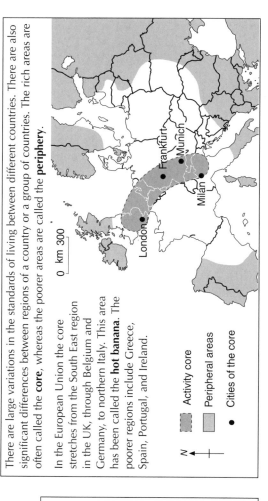

- Activity core
- Peripheral areas
- • Cities of the core

The richer areas, such as the South East in England, grow because
1 in the beginning they have **initial advantages**, such as more resources or a better location, or both
2 as they grow, they develop **acquired advantages** such as a skilled labour force, a marketing network, more industries, and investment.

By contrast, the peripheral areas decline. Their younger, more skilled workers migrate to the core in search of work. The periphery falls further behind the core.

Regional inequalities can be measured in a number of ways, including
- unemployment rates
- migration rates
- number of people owning their own home
- percentage of people staying on at school after GCSEs
- percentage of jobs in agriculture or manufacturing
- cost of land per hectare
- amount of regional aid from the government.

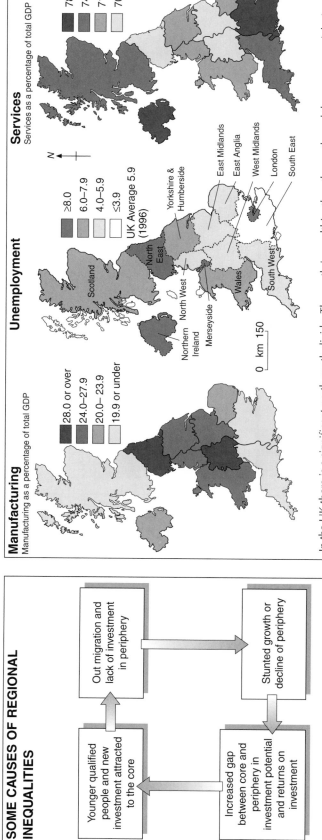

Manufacturing
Manufacturing as a percentage of total GDP

- 28.0 or over
- 24.0–27.9
- 20.0–23.9
- 19.9 or under

Unemployment

- ≥8.0
- 6.0–7.9
- 4.0–5.9
- ≤3.9

UK Average 5.9 (1996)

Scotland
Northern Ireland
North West
Merseyside
North East
Yorkshire & Humberside
East Midlands
East Anglia
West Midlands
Wales
London
South West
South East

0 km 150

Services
Services as a percentage of total GDP

- 78.0 or over
- 74.0–77.9
- 71.0–73.9
- 70.9 or under

In the UK there is a significant north-south divide. The south is wealthier than the north, and there are more jobs in service industries, and less unemployment. By contrast, the north has higher unemployment, and there are more jobs in manufacturing industries, and agriculture.

SOME CAUSES OF REGIONAL INEQUALITIES

Out migration and lack of investment in periphery

→ Stunted growth or decline of periphery

→ Increased gap between core and periphery in investment potential and returns on investment

→ Younger qualified people and new investment attracted to the core

Water resources

THE WATER PROBLEM

The world's water problem is serious and getting worse:

- two billion people lack access to safe water and three billion lack effective sanitation
- 40% of the world's population face chronic water shortages
- dirty water in LDCs causes 80% of illnesses, killing 10 million people annually.
- by 2030 there will be nearly 3 billion more people in the world
- by 2025 up to two-thirds of the world's population will lack sufficient water
- water shortages will slow down economic growth
- in the future, water shortages will be the biggest constraint on agriculture.

CHINA'S WATER SHORT FALL

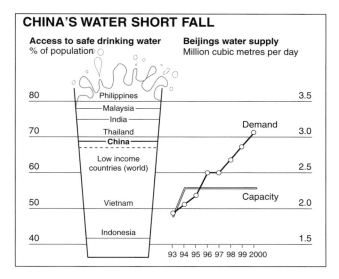

Access to safe drinking water
% of population

Beijings water supply
Million cubic metres per day

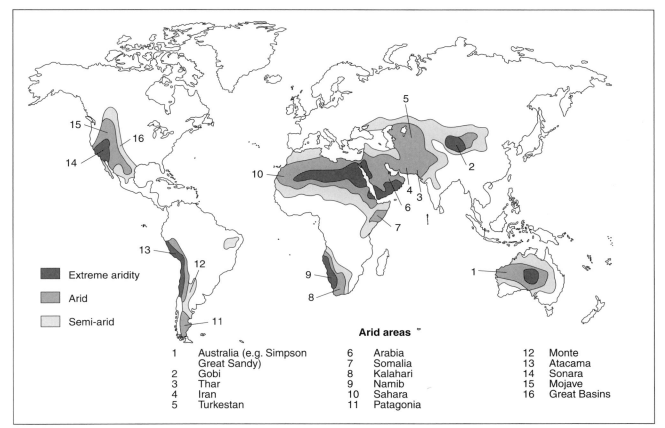

		Arid areas				
1	Australia (e.g. Simpson Great Sandy)	6	Arabia	12	Monte
2	Gobi	7	Somalia	13	Atacama
3	Thar	8	Kalahari	14	Sonara
4	Iran	9	Namib	15	Mojave
5	Turkestan	10	Sahara	16	Great Basins
		11	Patagonia		

Legend:
- Extreme aridity
- Arid
- Semi-arid

ACCESS TO WATER

In developing countries, one of the greatest environmental threats is that to water. Today, the world's supply of water is only one-third of what it was in 1970. Water scarcity is increasingly becoming a factor in ethnic strife and political tension. In 1990, about 1.3 billion people in the developing world lacked access to clean water. Much water pollution is the result of poor sanitation (nearly two billion people lack access to safe sanitation).

Percentage of population	1975–80		1990	
	Rural	Urban	Rural	Urban
with access to safe water	33	72	64	75
without access to safe water	67	28	36	25

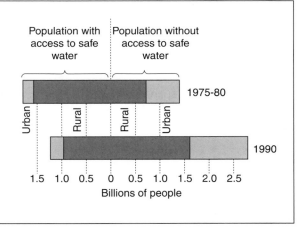

Population with access to safe water | Population without access to safe water

Billions of people

Water development schemes

The Three Gorges Dam will be one of the biggest dams in the world. Like most other large-scale developments, it has raised a number of issues. These can be divided into two: the advantages and the disadvantages. But first some facts:

* the Three Gorges Dam will be over 2km long and 100m high
* the lake will be over 600km long
* it will take between 15 and 20 years to build and could cost as much as $70 billion
* the Yangtze provides 66% of China's rice and contains 400m people
* the Yangtze drains 1.8m km² and discharges 700 cubic kilometres of water annually

THE ADVANTAGES

* it will generate up to 18,000 megawatts, eight times more than the Aswan Dam in Egypt and 50% more than the world's largest existing HEP dam
* it will enable China to reduce its dependency on coal
* it will supply Shanghai (population over 13m), one of the world's largest cities, and Chongqing (population 3m), an area earmarked for economic development with power
* it will protect 10m people from flooding (over 300,000 people in China have died as a result of flooding this century)
* it will allow shipping above the Three Gorges: the dams will raise water levels by 90m, and turn the rapids in the gorge into a lake

THE DISADVANTAGES

* most floods in recent years have come from rivers which join the Yangtze below the Three Gorges Dam
* the region is seismically active and landslides are frequent
* the port at the head of the lake may become silted up as a result of increased deposition and the development of a delta at the head of the lake
* up to 1.2m people will have to be moved to make way for the dam and the lake
* much of the land available for resettlement is over 800m above sea level, and is colder with infertile thin soils and on relatively steep slopes
* dozens of towns, for example Wanxian and Fuling with 140,000 and 80,000 people respectively, will be flooded
* up to 530m tonnes of silt are carried through the Gorge annually: the first dam on the river lost its capacity within seven years and one on the Yellow River filled with silt within four years
* to reduce the silt load, afforestation is needed, but resettlement of people will cause greater pressure on the slopes above the dam
* the dam will interfere with aquatic life – the Siberian Crane and the White Flag Dolphin are threatened with extinction
* archaeological treasures will be drowned, including the Zhang Fei temple

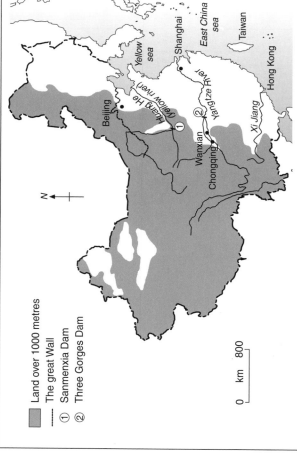

Land over 1000 metres
The great Wall
① Sanmenxia Dam
② Three Gorges Dam

0 km 800

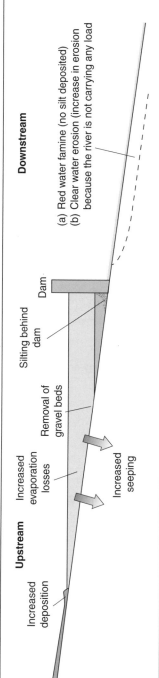

Upstream   Downstream

Increased deposition

Increased evaporation losses

Removal of gravel beds

Increased seeping

Silting behind dam

Dam

(a) Red water famine (no silt deposited)
(b) Clear water erosion (increase in erosion because the river is not carrying any load)

Disease

In MDCs most deaths are the result of cancers, heart diseases, and strokes. These are called **degenerative** diseases. By contrast, in LDCs most deaths are the result of diseases such as diarrhoea and vomiting, respiratory diseases, malaria, measles, and cholera. These are known as **infectious** or **contagious** diseases.

Deaths due to selected infectious diseases, 1995 estimates

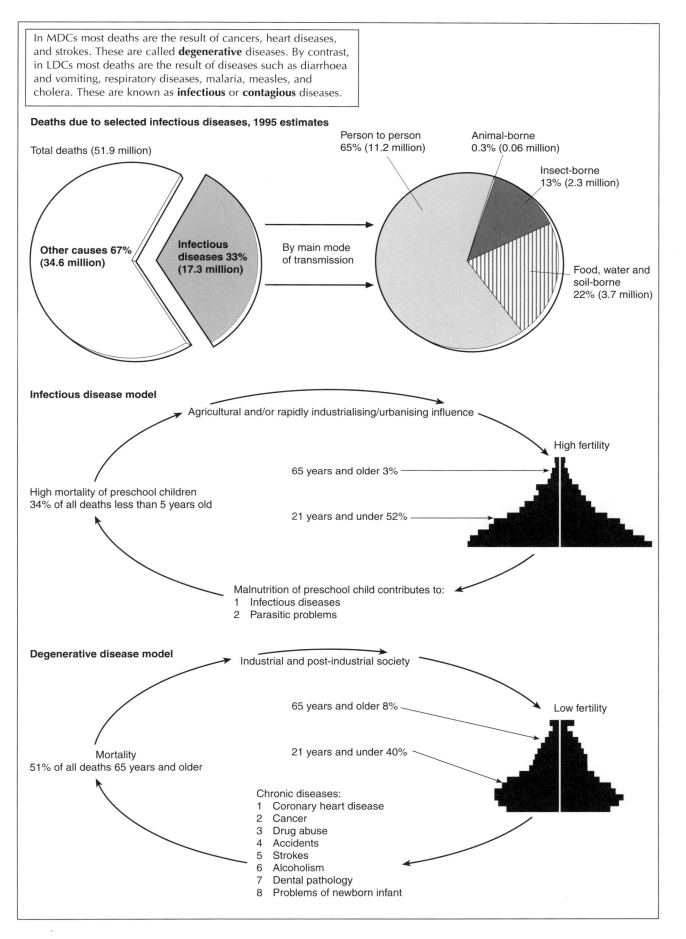

Total deaths (51.9 million)

Other causes 67% (34.6 million)

Infectious diseases 33% (17.3 million)

By main mode of transmission

Person to person 65% (11.2 million)

Animal-borne 0.3% (0.06 million)

Insect-borne 13% (2.3 million)

Food, water and soil-borne 22% (3.7 million)

Infectious disease model

Agricultural and/or rapidly industrialising/urbanising influence

High fertility

65 years and older 3%

21 years and under 52%

High mortality of preschool children 34% of all deaths less than 5 years old

Malnutrition of preschool child contributes to:
1   Infectious diseases
2   Parasitic problems

Degenerative disease model

Industrial and post-industrial society

Low fertility

65 years and older 8%

21 years and under 40%

Mortality 51% of all deaths 65 years and older

Chronic diseases:
1   Coronary heart disease
2   Cancer
3   Drug abuse
4   Accidents
5   Strokes
6   Alcoholism
7   Dental pathology
8   Problems of newborn infant

Disease 2

MALARIA

Insect-borne disease: malaria

Malaria kills up to 3 million people each year. Up to 40% of the world's population is at risk. Most of these are in sub-Sahara Africa. About 500 million more people suffer from the disease. As increasing numbers of people travel, they move into areas where malaria is present. The disease is affecting new victims because

- many people are not immune to the disease
- mosquitoes are becoming more drug resistant
- mosquitoes are spreading into areas previously free of the insect
- of expanding agricultural schemes
- of irrigation schemes
- of increasing international travel and trade.

As yet there is no accepted vaccine. In southern Tanzania up to 80% of the children are infected with the disease by the age of 6 months, and 4% of children under the age of 5 die as a result of malaria. Pregnant women, travellers, and refugees are also very vulnerable to the disease.

CONDITIONS FOR MALARIA

- mosquitoes need still water in which to lay their eggs
- temperatures of >16°c are required for the parasite to develop within the mosquito
- above 32°C large numbers of the parasites die
- malaria can cause fever, sweating, anaemia, and death

Global distribution of malaria, 1992

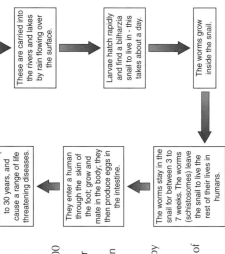

- Malaria present
- Malaria absent

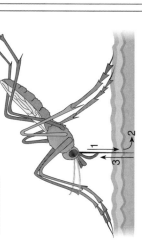

1. Proboscis of female mosquito enters bloodstream through skin

2. Saliva pours into the victim's blood to prevent clotting. Plasmodium parasites enter bloodstream

3. Blood sucked into stomach of female mosquito

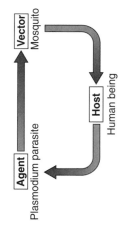

Vector Mosquito

Host Human being

Agent Plasmodium parasite

Diseases transmitted by contaminated water and food

DIARRHOEAL DISEASES

- these caused over 3 million deaths in 1995
- 80% were in children under the age of 5
- up to 70% of diarrhoea is caused by contaminated food
- in the USA in 1995 over 400, 000 people in Milwaukee were infected by contaminated water

SCHISTOSOMIASIS

This is also known as bilharzia. It causes chronic ill-health.

- about 200 million people are infected
- up to 600 million are at risk of the disease
- it is transmitted in stagnant water by parasitic worms, called schistosomes
- schistosome eggs are released by human faeces
- they grow in a snail called the bilharzia snail
- when they have developed within the snail they leave it and seek a human host
- they penetrate the skin and enter the bloodstream
- female worms lay hundreds of eggs daily for up to five years
- the eggs damage the intestine, bladder and other organs
- the disease kills 20 000 each year and also causes bladder cancer
- bladder cancer is the main cause of death in Egyptian males under the age of 44 years
- the disease is spread by large-scale dams and irrigation which increases the amount of stagnant water

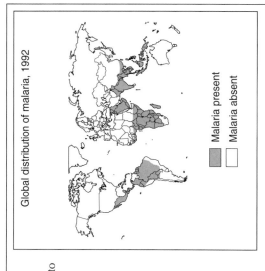

When someone excretes in the open, worms' eggs may be passed out in the excrement.

These are carried into the rivers and lakes by rain flowing over the surface.

Larvae hatch rapidly and find a bilharzia snail to live in - this takes about a day.

The worms grow inside the snail.

The worms stay in the snail for between 3 to 7 weeks. The worms (schistosomes) leave the snail to live the rest of their lives in humans.

They enter a human through the skin of the foot; grow and mate in the body; they then produce eggs in the intestine.

Worms can live for up to 30 years, and cause a range of life threatening diseases.

Types of development

TOP-DOWN DEVELOPMENT

- this is usually large-scale
- carried out by governments, international organisations, and 'experts'
- it is done by people from outside the area
- it is imposed upon the area or people by outside organisations
- it is often well funded and can respond quickly to disasters
- the Three Gorges Dam and the Aswan High Dam are good examples of top down development
- the local people are not involved in the decision making process
- emergency relief can also be considered top down

BOTTOM-UP

- this is small-scale
- it involves local communities and local people
- it is labour intensive
- there is usually limited funding available
- common projects include building earthen dams, creating cottage industries
- the local people are involved in the decision making process
- it is run by the locals for the locals

NON-GOVERNMENT ORGANISATIONS

- these include Oxfam, Save the Children, Cafod
- they are mostly charities
- they are not allied to any political party
- NGOs normally work with local communities and small-groups
- they also help with emergency relief (short-term disaster relief)

SUSTAINABLE DEVELOPMENT

- this is development which safeguards natural resources for future generations
- it aims at increasing standards of living without destroying the environment
- it aims to satisfy basic needs such as food supply and water, rather than large-scale developments which may be inappropriate
- it reduces waste
- it increases efficiency and recycling

APPROPRIATE DEVELOPMENT

- development which is culturally acceptable, technologically understandable, and economically affordable
- it is for the community, by the community, with the community's own resources
- it is a type of bottom-up or sustainable form of development

MULTI-PURPOSE SCHEMES

- these have a number of aims
- a water scheme might include a mixture of water supply, flood relief, HEP, tourism, navigation, industrial development

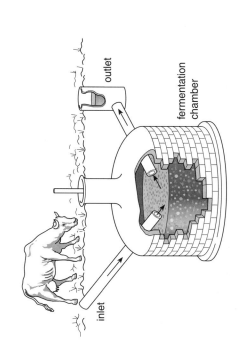

inlet

outlet

fermentation chamber

Biogas plants are used in over 50 LDCs. They are an appropriate, sustainable type of development which provides fuel and fertiliser. All forms of waste are fed into fermentation cylinders to produce methane gas. This provides the energy. The remains can be used as fertiliser.

Trade

Trade is the import (buying) and export (selling) of goods such as food, fuel, manufactured goods, raw materials, finance, and technology.

The balance of trade is the difference in money terms between imports and exports
- a positive balance of trade means that exports cost more than imports
- a negative balance of trade means that imports cost more than exports.

Free trade allows a country to trade with any other country in a competitive manner. By contrast, protectionism restricts trade between countries. Protectionism includes
- taxes or tariffs on imports
- different national currencies
- quotas on imports

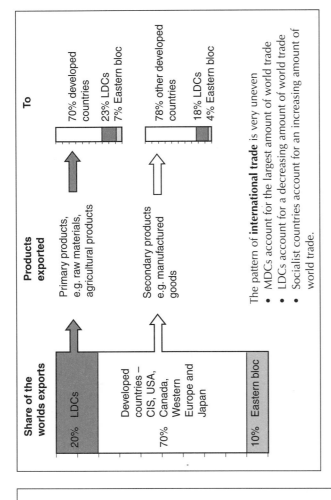

Manufactured processed goods → Import → Less developed country → Export → Raw materials, agricultural goods

Links between developed and less developed countries

Developed country ← Import ← Raw materials, agricultural goods

Export ← Developed country

MDCs and LDCs have different export and import patterns. MDCs mostly export machinery, transport equipment, chemicals, and services. Their range of imports is similar. By contrast, LDCs have a much smaller range of exports - these are mostly agricultural products and raw materials. Their range of imports is similar to MDCs but is likely to be cheaper and less sophisticated.

Share of the worlds exports

20%	LDCs
70%	Developed countries – CIS, USA, Canada, Western Europe and Japan
10%	Eastern bloc

Products exported

Primary products, e.g. raw materials, agricultural products

Secondary products e.g. manufactured goods

To

70% developed countries
23% LDCs
7% Eastern bloc

78% other developed countries
18% LDCs
4% Eastern bloc

The pattern of **international trade** is very uneven
- MDCs account for the largest amount of world trade
- LDCs account for a decreasing amount of world trade
- Socialist countries account for an increasing amount of world trade.

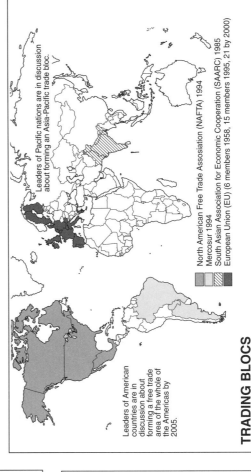

Leaders of American countries are in discussion about forming a free trade area of the whole of the Americas by 2005.

Leaders of Pacific nations are in discussion about forming an Asia-Pacific trade bloc.

North American Free Trade Assosiation (NAFTA) 1994
Mercosur 1994
South Asian Association for Economic Cooperation (SAARC) 1985
European Union (EU) (6 members 1958, 15 members 1995, 21 by 2000)

TRADING BLOCS

A trading bloc is a group of countries which protect their industries and markets. They allow free trade within the trading bloc, and they place restrictions on the amount of imports from other countries. For members of the trading bloc there are two main advantages
1 they have access to a large market, in the case of the EU 370 million people
2 they protect industries against foreign competitors.

Trading partners 1992/3

Europe
Americas
Africa
Asia
Oceania

USA   Mexico

IMPORTS

EXPORTS

Aid

Aid is any help or assistance given to improve the quality of life of the receiver. It includes money, equipment, goods, staff, and services. Most aid is from MDCs to LDCs but there is aid to the poorer regions in MDCs. For example, Northern Ireland and Scotland receive much **regional aid** from the EU, and parts of Croatia and Bosnia receive aid from the United Nations.

Aid to LDCs is often divided into
- short-term aid or emergency relief
- long-term aid.

There are three main forms of aid.

1 **Bilateral** aid - when one country gives to another country. Often the MDC uses it to its own advantage, so that it can dictate the conditions of aid. There are political ties between the countries.

2 **Multilateral** - when more than one country gives aid to a number of countries. The amount of aid to each country may be quite low, and the interest rates are often very high.

3 **Charities** - such as Cafod, Save the Children, and Oxfam. The moneys involved are small by comparison to bilateral and multilateral aid but there are no political ties. Charities work independently from governments and they are called **non-government organisations**.

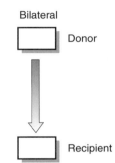

From one country direct to another country
55% of British aid is bilateral

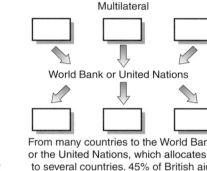

From many countries to the World Bank or the United Nations, which allocates it to several countries. 45% of British aid is multilateral

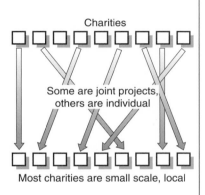

Most charities are small scale, local

The amount of aid given varies between countries. The United Nations suggest that most countries donate up to 1% of GNP. However, only Norway and Sweden reach this target.

The largest donors are the USA, France, Germany, and the UK. The UK donates nearly £2 billion to over 150 countries.

Aid money is spent on a number of schemes such as
- health care
- education
- water and sanitation
- agricultural development

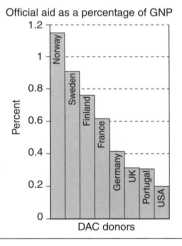

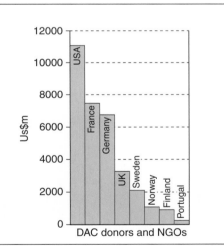

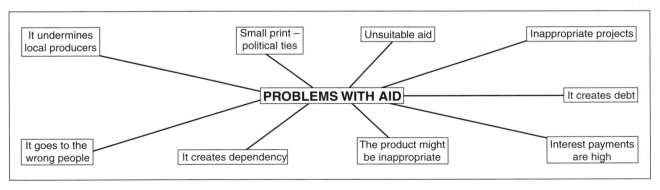

Tourism in Europe

Tourism is now one of the world's largest industries. The number of foreign holidays rose from approximately 25 million in 1950 to over 350 million in the mid-1990s. The World Travel Organisation (WTO) estimates that nearly 500 million foreign holidays are taken each year, and that the number of holidays at home is even greater.

The rise in tourism has had a serious effect on many countries - not just economically but in terms of social effects and environmental damage. Although most of the global pattern of tourism is between MDCs, many LDCs are turning towards tourism as a way to develop and as a means of securing foreign income.

The main destinations in the United Kingdom can be divided into six main overlapping types:

1 coastal, e.g. Blackpool, and North Wales
2 scenic landscapes, e.g. Scotland, and Northern Ireland
3 mountainous and ski centres, e.g. the Lake District, and the Cairngorms
4 capital cities and heritage centres e.g. London, York, and Oxford
5 leisure centres, e.g. Alton Towers, Legoland, and Center Parcs
6 Business-conference centres, e.g. NEC, Birmingham

The rise in tourism is related to a number of economic and social trends:

- increased leisure time
- cheaper, faster forms of transport, especially the Transatlantic aircraft
- an increase in income and standards of living
- a broadening of lifestyle expectations
- the growth of the package holiday
- greater media exposure, travel programmes etc.
- a rise in the number of second holidays, short breaks etc.

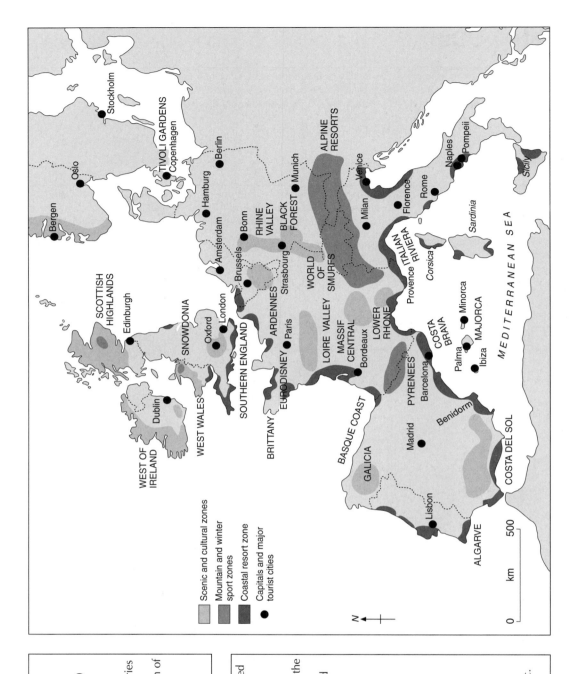

Scenic and cultural zones

Mountain and winter sport zones

Coastal resort zone

● Capitals and major tourist cities

Tourism in LDCs

Tourists are attracted to developing countries, such as South Africa, Kenya, and Sierra Leone for a number of reasons. South Africa, for example, is rapidly becoming a destination for foreign visitors for a variety of reasons:

1 its rich and varied wildlife and world famous game reserves, e.g. Kruger National Park
2 a tropical climate, which is attractive for European visitors, especially in December-January
3 glorious beaches in Natal
4 a rich cultural heritage and tradition of the Zulu, Xhosa and Sotho peoples
5 it is relatively cheap compared to developed countries (£1 = Rand 7)
6 English is widely spoken and there are many links with the UK
7 it is perceived as a safe destination since the collapse of Apartheid and the election of the new ANC government.

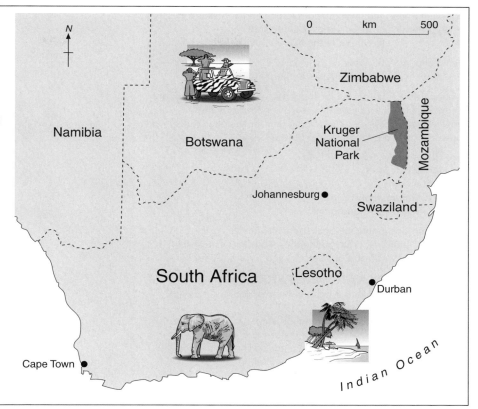

There are a number of **benefits** which tourism can bring to a developing economy, such as that of South Africa

1 **Foreign currency**: the number of foreign tourists has increased by 15% per annum during the 1990s and contributes 3.2% of South Africa's gross domestic product (GDP)
2 **Employment**: thousands are employed in formal (registered) and informal (unregistered) occupations ranging from hotels, and tour operators to cleaners, gardeners, and souvenir hawkers
3 It is a more **profitable** way to use semi-arid grassland: estimates of the annual returns per hectare of land range from R60-80 for pastoralism to R250 for dry-land farming and R1, 000 for game parks and tourism
4 **Investment**: over R5 billion was invested in South Africa's tourist infrastructure in 1995, upgrading hotels, airlines, car rental fleets, roads etc.

However, there are a number of problems that have arisen as a result of the tourist industry:

1 Undue pressure on natural ecosystems, leading to soil erosion, litter pollution, decline of animal numbers
2 Much tourist-related employment is unskilled, seasonal, part-time, poorly paid, and lacking any rights for the workers
3 Resources are spent on providing for tourists while local people may have to go without
4 A large proportion of the profits go to overseas companies, tour operators, hotel chains etc.
5 Crime is increasingly directed at tourists; much is petty crime but there have been very serious incidents, e.g. rape
6 Tourism is by nature very unpredictable, varying with the strength of the economy, cost, safety, alternative opportunities, stage in the family life-cycle and so on.

ECOTOURISM

Ecotourism refers to any form of tourism where the primary attraction is an ecosystem such as a game reserve, coral reef, mountain or forest park etc. It has recently been widened to include 'primitive' indigenous people. It is widely perceived as the acceptable form of tourism and that it is a form of sustainable development, i.e. a type of tourism that can be developed without any ill-effects on the natural environment. However, much that passes for ecotourism is merely an expensive package holiday that has been cleverly marketed with the 'eco' label.

Ecotourism developed as a form of specialised, flexible tourism. It emerged because mass tourism was seen as having a negative impact upon natural and social environment, and also because there was a growing number of wealthy tourists dissatisfied with package holidays. In the original sense, people who took an 'ecotourism' holiday were prepared to accept quite simple accommodation and facilities. This is sustainable and has little effect upon the environment. However, as a location becomes more popular and is marketed more, the number of tourists increases causing more accommodation and improved facilities to be built, e.g. more hotels with showers, baths and air conditioning, bars, sewage facilities etc. This is an unsustainable form of ecotourism as it destroys part of the environment and/or culture that visitors choose to visit.

The impact of tourism

National Parks were introduced into England and Wales in 1949
- to preserve and enhance the countryside and
- to promote enjoyment of the National Parks by the public.

Ten National Parks were designated in 1955 and they are now managed by the National Parks Authority (NPA).

National Parks are run by local boards, committees and county councils. One-third of the Board are appointed by the government. However, much of the land in National Parks is privately owned by farmers and others.

The duties of the NPA include to
- gain access for the public
- plant woodlands
- set up information centres
- provide car parks and picnic sites.

Interest groups in the National Parks include Farmers, Landlords, Water authorities, Forestry Commission, National Trust, Ministry of Defence, and County Councils.

PROBLEMS IN NATIONAL PARKS
- honeypot sites - increasing numbers of visitors destroy the sites they come to see
- landowners - do not like people roaming over their land
- visitors want car parks, visitor centres and so on
- crops get trampled on, gates are left open
- congestion leads to noise and air pollution
- second homes cause an increase in local house prices
- agricultural developments remove dry stone walls, heathlands, hedgerows, meadows and woodlands

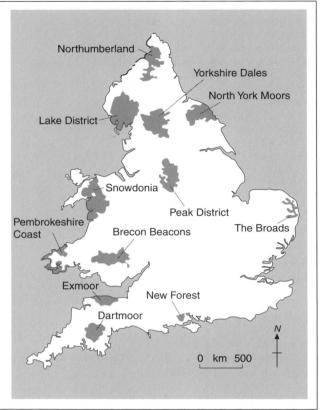

THE CONFLICTS ON DARTMOOR

Population growth increases demand for housing which increases demand for building materials, more roads and so on.

China clay is mined from granite for industry. Quarries need access roads and are heavily polluted by dust and noise, spoil heaps and water pollution.

Afforestation schemes usually replace deciduous woodland with coniferous woodland. Coniferous woodlands are quite 'plain' compared to deciduous ones. For example, oak trees support about 400 types of insect whereas spruce trees support only 3.

Demands for recreation include water sports, walking, pony-trekking, mountain biking, hang gliding, bird watching and so on. All of these require improved access roads, more facilities, more pollution and so on.

Tourism brings in a great deal of money but creates noise, litter, and pollution. The Dartmoor NPA tries to reduce the conflict by **land use zoning,** that is attracting visitors to some areas (by providing car parks and other facilities) and keeping them away from other places (by not providing facilities).

Dartmoor is also used by the army. This causes soil erosion (by tanks) and the disturbance to many birds and animals due to the firing ranges on Dartmoor. On the other hand, the Ministry of Defence keep large areas free from visitors so valuable landscapes are protected.

Dartmoor National Park receives over 8 million visits each year.

Farming has an impact on the environment. Overstocking causes vegetation removal and soil erosion.

Because granite is hard and impermeable, it makes a good site for reservoirs. But lakes drown out natural habitats.

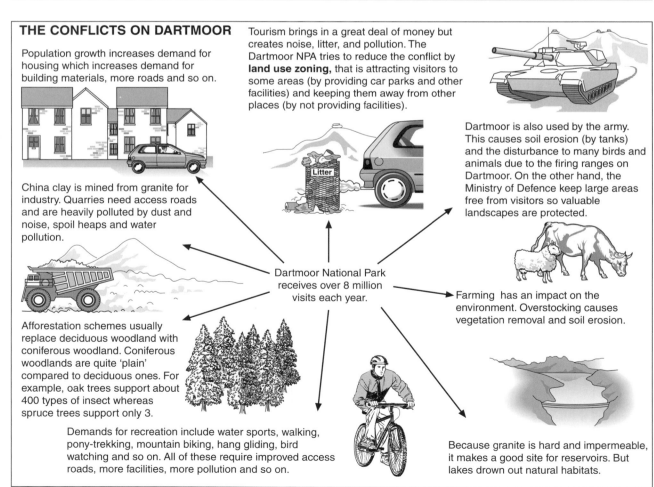

Test section

Answering questions
The type of answer depends upon the type of question. For example the question may ask you to
- list
- describe
- explain
- evaluate
- compare
- contrast.

This is in addition to all the skills-type questions that can be asked.

For example, the question 'List the factors why Oxford is prone to flooding' requires only a list of points such as
- Oxford is low lying
- two major rivers meet there
- human activity has increased the risk of flooding
- the local geology is impermeable

By contrast, a question which says 'Describe the flood problem in Oxford' looks for more detail and the use of local information. It is also asking for full sentences. An answer might read

'Oxford is affected by the flooding of the River Thames and the River Cherwell. The Cherwell now floods more often due to human activity; and the Thames floods on Port Meadow most winters. The areas at risk of flooding are along the banks of both rivers. Occasional flash floods occur in Summer, but it is the flooding by the rivers in areas close by that is the main problem in Oxford. Most of this land is now used for sports grounds, farmland, and recreation.

If the question is 'Explain the flood problem in Oxford.' the answer requires explanation, examples and full sentences. An answer might read

'Oxford suffers from many floods because two main rivers meet there. This means there is a lot of water passing through a small area. In addition, much of the area is covered by clay. Clay is an impermeable rock, which means that water does not sink into the rock but flows over the surface. Therefore, in Oxford water flows over the land and increases the risk of flooding. Also, a large part of the area is covered by concrete. So much of the rain flows over the surface and into the storm sewers and drains. This increases the problem of flooding.

'Evaluate the problem of flooding in Oxford.' This question asks us to compare the problem of flooding in Oxford with other areas, and to assess how important flooding is in Oxford. For example,

'Flooding in Oxford is an increasing problem. Human activity, such as the building of houses, bridges, deforestation in agricultural areas, and so on, is increasing the amount of water that reaches the rivers. To cope with the problem, land use zoning or management has been developed. In general, close to the rivers (i.e. the areas liable to flood) land is given over to farming (Cherwell Valley), recreation (Port Meadow) and sports grounds (Magdalene College playing fields). But compared to places such as the Ganges Delta, Oxford's flood problem is not very serious. It causes economic disruption but it does not lead to a loss of life or a loss of property.

Weather maps

Weather map showing path of a low pressure system

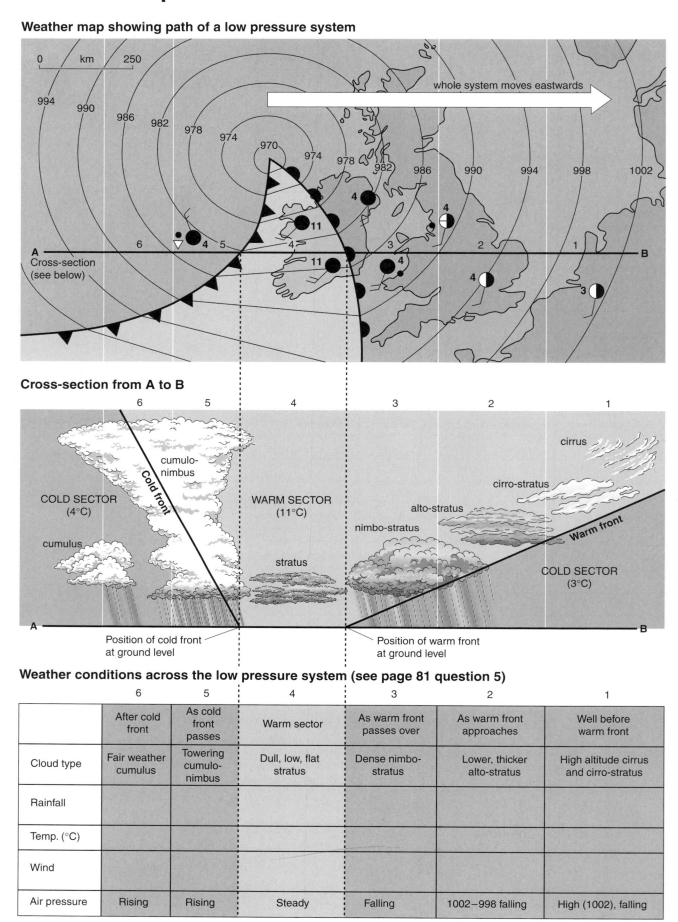

whole system moves eastwards

Cross-section from A to B

Weather conditions across the low pressure system (see page 81 question 5)

	6	5	4	3	2	1
	After cold front	As cold front passes	Warm sector	As warm front passes over	As warm front approaches	Well before warm front
Cloud type	Fair weather cumulus	Towering cumulo-nimbus	Dull, low, flat stratus	Dense nimbo-stratus	Lower, thicker alto-stratus	High altitude cirrus and cirro-stratus
Rainfall						
Temp. (°C)						
Wind						
Air pressure	Rising	Rising	Steady	Falling	1002−998 falling	High (1002), falling

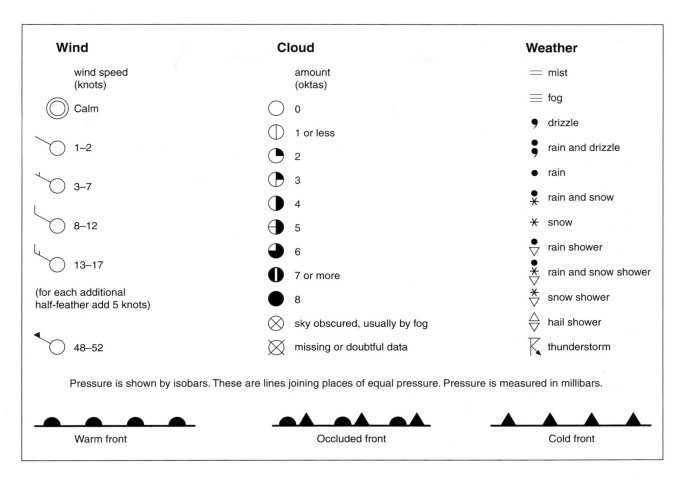

Wind	Cloud	Weather

Wind

wind speed (knots)

Calm

1–2

3–7

8–12

13–17

(for each additional half-feather add 5 knots)

48–52

Cloud

amount (oktas)

0

1 or less

2

3

4

5

6

7 or more

8

sky obscured, usually by fog

missing or doubtful data

Weather

mist

fog

drizzle

rain and drizzle

rain

rain and snow

snow

rain shower

rain and snow shower

snow shower

hail shower

thunderstorm

Pressure is shown by isobars. These are lines joining places of equal pressure. Pressure is measured in millibars.

Warm front

Occluded front

Cold front

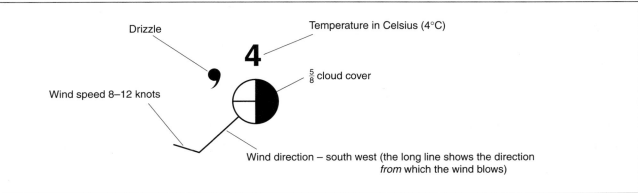

Drizzle

Temperature in Celsius (4°C)

$\frac{5}{8}$ cloud cover

Wind speed 8–12 knots

Wind direction – south west (the long line shows the direction *from* which the wind blows)

Questions

Study the weather map, cross section through the depression, table of weather conditions, and the key for weather symbols. Answer the following questions.

1 What type of weather system is shown in the diagram?

2 What type of front passes through Ireland?

3 Describe the weather conditions in

   a) Southern England?

   b) South West Ireland?

4 Study the cross-section of the depression. Describe how the clouds change as the fronts pass over.

5 Complete the table showing the weather conditions at points along the cross-section A–B.

Map skills

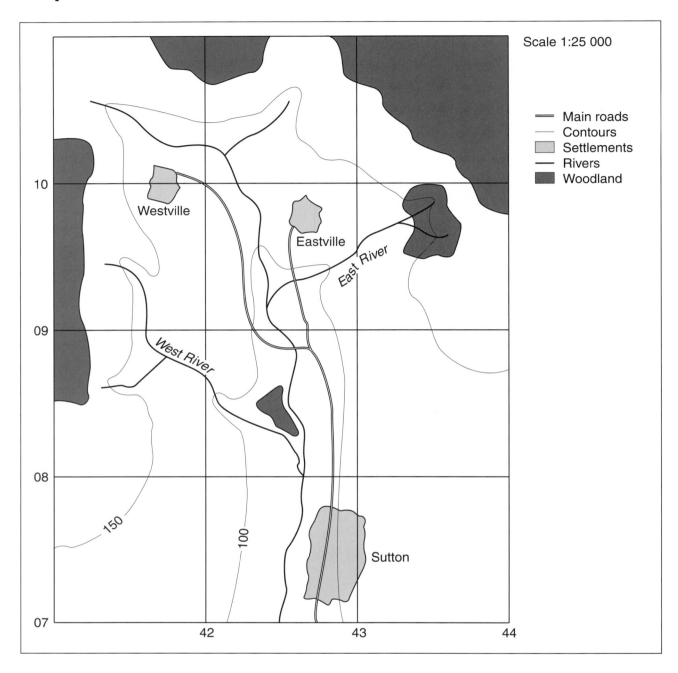

Scale 1:25 000

Legend:
- ═══ Main roads
- ── Contours
- ▨ Settlements
- ── Rivers
- ▦ Woodland

Westville

Eastville

East River

West River

150

100

Sutton

Questions

1 What is the distance, to the nearest kilometre, between Sutton and Eastville?

2 On a 1:25 000 map, how many centimetres represent one kilometre?

3 What direction is Eastville from Sutton?

4 Give the four-figure square reference for Eastville.

5 Give the six-figure grid reference for the point where the West River meets the East River.

6 Describe the site of Eastville.

7 Draw a cross section from 410090 to 440090 to show drainage (rivers) and communications (roads). The base has already been drawn for you (page 83).

8 In the grid provided on page 83, draw the woodland and rivers. The contours have been put on for you.

9 Describe the distribution of woodland as shown on the map.

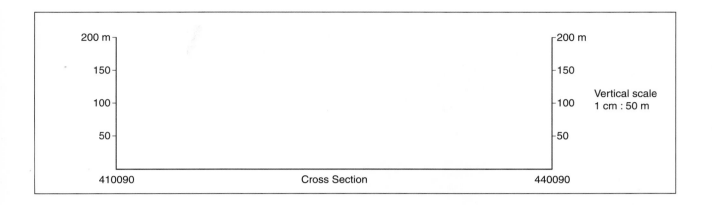

200 m ⌐   200 m ⌐
150 ⊢   150 ⊢
100 ⊢   Vertical scale   100 ⊢
                               1 cm : 50 m
50 ⊢   50 ⊢

410090   Cross Section   440090

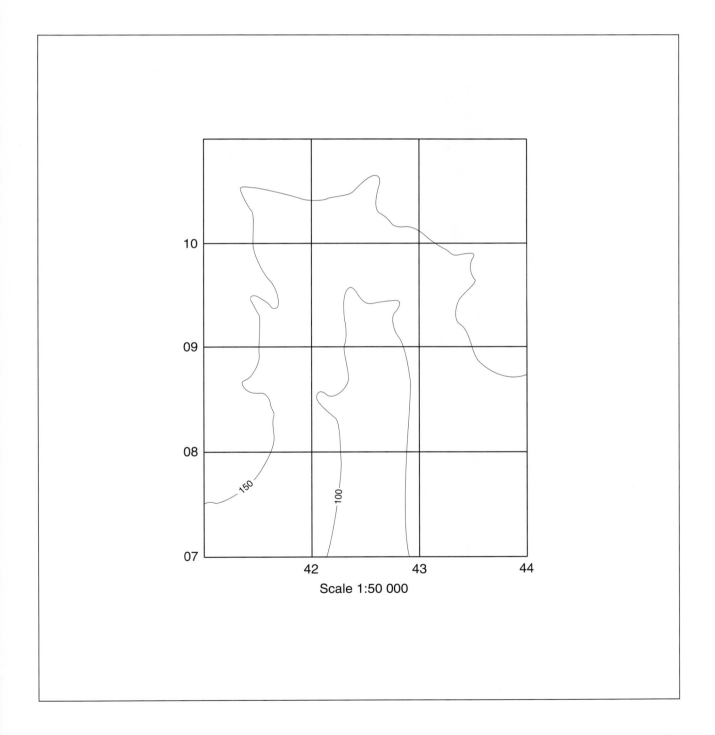

10

09

08

07

                    42   43   44

Scale 1:50 000

Test section 83

Annotated photographs

Physical landscapes

The photograph shows a small mountain stream. On the sketch diagram below, label the following:

1 bare exposed rock

2 scree slope

3 low angle, vegetated (grassy) slope

4 wide, shallow river

5 large boulder

Annotated photographs

Human landscapes

The photograph below shows part of a large urban area. On the sketch diagram below, label the following:

1 urban motorway

2 elevated railway

3 parkland

4 high rise commercial buildings

Test questions

(pages 1–9)

Geology and rocks (pages 1–9)
1 Give an example of a Mid Ocean Ridge and a subduction zone.
2 What happens at a subduction zone?
3 List three factors which may cause an earthquake.
4 Define the terms metamorphic, igneous and sedimentary.
5 What is meant by the term weathering. Describe how either freeze-thaw or carbonation-solution takes place.
6 Give two reasons to explain why limestone scenery is unique.
7 Describe the main features associated with chalk landscapes.
8 What is a tor? With the use of a sketch diagram, explain how tors are formed.
9 In what ways are rocks useful to people. Use examples to support your answer.

Rivers and hydrology (pages 10–14)
10 What is meant by the term 'the hydrological cycle'?
11 What is a river regime?
12 Draw an annotated (labelled) diagram to show a flood hydrograph.
13 With the use of diagrams, explain how waterfalls are formed.
14 With the use of diagrams, explain how either levees or ox-bow lakes are formed.
15 With the use of examples explain how (**a**) rivers have affected human activity and (**b**) how human activity has affected rivers.

Glaciers (pages 15–20)
16 List three factors that affect the rate of glacial erosion.
17 With the use of an annotated diagram, explain how corries are formed.
18 List two features of glacial deposition.
19 With the use of examples, explain how glacial landscapes have been used by people.

Coasts (pages 21–25)
20 Define the terms fetch, swash and backwash.
21 What is meant by the term long shore drift?
22 With the use of examples, state the difference between spits, bars and tombolos.
23 Briefly explain 4 types of erosion that take place in coastal areas.
24 What are the problems associated with the human use of coastal areas?
25 For an area of coastline that you have studied, evaluate the successfulness of methods of coastal protection.

Study the diagram which shows a plan view of a coastline which is being actively eroded.

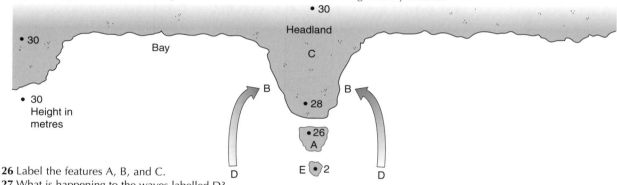

26 Label the features A, B, and C.
27 What is happening to the waves labelled D?
28 In what way are the waves D affecting the headland?

Study the map which shows long shore drift on part of the British coastline.

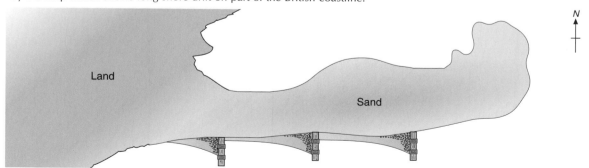

29 What direction is long shore drift occurring on the map?
30 Give two pieces of contrasting evidence to support your answer.

Climate (pages 26–29)

31 List three ways in which tropical climates differ from temperate ones.

32 Briefly explain two factors which affect temperature.

33 List three types of rainfall. Explain how any one of these operates.

34 What is meant by the term 'the greenhouse effect'?

Soils (pages 30–34)

35 Explain how either climate or geology affects soil formation.

36 What do the terms leaching and gleying mean?

37 What type of soil would you expect to find in (**a**) warm temperate areas, such as lowland Britain, and (**b**) in cold temperate areas such as Sweden and Norway.

38 With the use of examples explain how human activity affects soils.

Ecosystems (pages 35–39)

39 What is an ecosystem?

40 Under what climatic conditions are tropical rain forests found?

41 Describe the effect of human activity on tropical rain forests.

42 How does the vegetation in deciduous forests differ from that in coniferous forests?

43 How does the climate in deciduous forests differ from that in coniferous forests?

44 What is the main type of ecosystem found in
  a) the British Isles
  b) Indonesia and/or northern Brazil
  c) the Great Plains of the USA?

45 What are the temperature and rainfall requirements for hot deserts to form?

46 What type of soil is found in
  (**a**) a deciduous forest, and (**b**) a coniferous forest.

47 Study the diagram of the pond as an ecosystem. Give examples of
  (**a**) an autotroph (**b**) a herbivore and (**c**) a carnivore.

48 What type of animal is (**a**) a fox and (**b**) a rabbit?

49 Give two contrasting examples of (**a**) abiotic elements in a pond and
  (**b**) biotic elements in a pond.

50 In what type of country is most destruction of the rainforest taking place?

51 Why is there so much erosion of rainforest soils once the vegetation has been removed?

52 How is vegetation in a coniferous forest adapted to climate?

53 How do deciduous trees adapt to cold winters?

Population (pages 40–44)

54 Explain the terms distribution and density of population.

55 What is the dependency ratio?

56 For any country that you have studied, describe and explain its distribution of population.

57 Why are birth rates higher in developing countries than in developed countries?

58 List five ways of increasing the amount of food per person in the developing world.

59 For an area that you have studied, describe and explain the impact of migration on either the area from which people moved or the area to which they went.

Settlement (pages 45–52)

60 Explain the terms site and situation.

61 Describe how the number and type of services changes with settlement size.

62 Describe how the pattern of commercial, industrial and residential land use varies with distance from a city centre.

63 What are the characteristics of a central business district (CBD)?

64 With the use of examples, describe the problems of inner city areas.

65 Using a diagram, show how new towns and green belts are related.

66 What are the problems associated with very large cities (supercities)?

67 For a city in the developing world that you have studied, describe its problems and the attempts to solve them.

Farming (pages 53–58)

68 Explain the terms extensive farming and intensive farming.

69 For any region in the UK, describe how farming activities are adapted to the physical environment.

70 List **two** advantages and **two** disadvantages of the Common Agricultural Policy (CAP).

71 Why is agriculture important in developing countries?

72 What is meant by the term 'the green revolution'? What effect has it had on developing countries?

73 Describe and account for any one environmental problem related to agriculture in the UK.

Industry (pages 59–65)
74 List five factors which affect the location of industry.
75 Where are the main world centres of car manufacturing?
76 What are the three main stages in the UK's iron and steel industry. What effect does this have on the location of new steel works?
77 Where, and why, are high technology industries found in the UK?
78 Describe the distribution of service employment in the UK.
79 What are the characteristics of a newly industrialising country (NIC)?
80 Briefly describe the effects of industrialisation of NICs.

Contrasts in development (pages 66–75)
81 What are the characteristics of (a) a developed country and (b) a less developed or developing country?
82 Name an MDC (A), an LDC (B), a CPE (C), an oil rich country (D) and an NIC (E).
83 Why are oil-rich countries given a special category of their own?
84 What kind of country is (a) the UK and (b) India.
85 Briefly explain the meaning of the terms gross national product (GNP), purchasing power parity (PPP), and human development index (HDI).
86 What three indicators are used to work out the HDI?
87 What type of countries have the highest HDI?
88 What is the HDI of
   (a) the UK and
   (b) India?
89 What is the infant mortality rate in (a) the UK and (b) India?
90 Why do regional contrasts (inequalities) occur? Use examples to support your answer.
91 What is the world's water problem?
92 How many people in developing countries do not have access to clean water?
93 How will the dam lead to a reduction in the emission of greenhouse gasses?
94 How many people have died in China in the twentieth century as a result of floods?
95 How long did it take for the lake on the Hwang He (Yellow River) to silt up?
96 Is the Three Gorges Dam a good thing or a bad thing? Justify your answer.
97 What do the terms 'red water famine' and 'clear water erosion' mean?
98 Distinguish between infectious (contagious) diseases and degenerative ones.
99 For any disease that you have studied, describe the impact it has on people and society.
100 What kind of water do mosquitoes need to lay their eggs?
101 What is the temperature range (maximum temperature and minimum temperature) that mosquitoes are found in?
102 What is the difference between (a) top-down and (b) bottom-up development?
103 Why is trade important to developing countries?
104 List four problems associated with aid.

Tourism and recreation (pages 76-78)
105 Explain why tourism has become one of the world's most important industries.
106 'Tourism is a mixed-blessing for ELDCs'. Using examples, discuss this statement.
107 What are the benefits of tourism to an area?
108 What are the main disadvantages of tourism to developing countries?
109 Briefly explain the main conflicts found in Britain's national parks, such as Dartmoor National Park.

INDEX

infectious disease 71
infiltration 10
inner city 49
intensive agriculture 53
intensive farming 53
interception 10
intrazonal soils 31
iron and steel 61
Japan 3, 60
joints 7

K

kame 19, 20
kettle hole 19, 20*
Kobe earthquake 3

L

latitude 27
latosols 33
LDCs see developing countries
leaching 32
levee 13
limestone 4, 6, 9, 31
location of industry 59
London 50
long shore drift 22, 24
low order goods 46

M

M4 Corridor 62
magma 2, 4
malaria 72
Malthus 43
management (coastal) 24-5
Mann 347
manufacturing industry 59
map skills 82
mechanical weathering 5
meltwater 15, 19
metamorphic 4
migration 44
MNCs 64
moraine 15, 18
Mount Pinatubo 7
Mount St. Helens 2
multilateral aid 75
multinational companies 64
multipurpose development 73

N

national parks 78
Netherlands - migration 44
new towns 50, 52
newly industrialising countries 64-5, 66
NGO 73
NICs 64-5, 66
nitrate pollution 58
non-government organisation 73
North Atlantic Drift 27
North-South divide 66

O

ocean currents 27
orographic rainfall 28
Otmoor 45
overland run off 10
ox-bow lakes 12
Oxford (flooding) 14

P

Pacific Ring of Fire 2
pastoral farming 53

peak flow 11
permeability 4
plate tectonics 1
plucking 16
podzolisation 32
podzols 33
population 40-4, 51
population and resources 42
population growth 42
population pyramids 40
pot holes 12
precipitation 10
pressure release 5
primacy 51
primary industry 59
primate cities 51
producer services 63
push-pull 44
pyramidal peak 17

Q

quaternary industry 59
quick flow 11

R

rain forest 35, 36-7
rainfall 28
range 46
raw materials 58
recessional limb 11
red-water famine 70
refraction 22
regimes 10
regional inequalities 68
relief 4
relief (and soils) 31
relief rainfall 28
rendzina 33
research and development 59
ribbon lake 17, 19
rising limb 11
rivers 10-4
roche moutonnee 17
rocks 4-9
rural settlements 45-6

S

salinisation 34
saltation 12
sand dune erosion 24
scarp slope 7
schistosomiasis 72
sea wall 25
secondary industry 59
sedimentary 4, 6, 7
services 63, 68
set-aside 55
settlement 45-52
shanty towns 52
sheep farming 54
shifting cultivation 37
Silicon Fen 62
Silicon Glen 62
site 45
situation 45
snout 15
soil compaction 34
soil erosion 34, 58
soil management 34
soils 30-4
solution 5, 12, 23

South Africa 40, 72
sphere of influence 46
spit 22
stack 23
stalactites 6
stalagmites 6
storm flow 11
storm hydrographs 10
structure (soil) 30
stump 23
sublimation 15
subsistence farming 53
supercities 51
suspension 12
sustainable development 73
swallow holes 6
swash 21, 22

T

temperature 27
tertiary industry 35
texture (soil) 30
Three Gorges Dam 70
threshold 46
time (and soils) 31
time lag 11
tombolo 22
top-down development 73
tors 7
tourism 76-8
Toyota 60
traction 12
trade 74
trading bloc 74
transport 59
trophic pyramid 35
tropical rain forest 35, 36-7
trough 17
truncated spur 17

U

U-shaped valley 17
UK 29, 40, 67
UK - distribution and density 41
unemployment 68
urban hydrographs 10
urban land use 47
urban problems 49, 52
urban redevelopment 49
USA 60

V

Vale of Evesham 54
village shape 45
villages 46
volcanoes 2

W

Wales 54
water (hydrological) cycle 10
water development schemes 70
water resources 69
waterfalls 12
wave cut platform 23
waves 10
weather maps 80-1
weather symbols 80
weathering 5, 23
winds 27

Z

Zambia - migration 44